THE
CHRONOLOGICAL
GUIDE TO BIBLE
PROPHECY

TODD HAMPSON

HARVEST PROPHECY
AN IMPRINT OF HARVEST HOUSE PUBLISHERS

Published in association with William K. Jensen Literary Agency, 119 Bampton Court, Eugene, Oregon, 97404

Cover design by Studio Gearbox, Chris Gilbert

Cover illustrations by Todd Hampson

Interior design by Chad Dougherty

For bulk, special sales, or ministry purchases, please call 1-800-547-8979. Email: Customerservice@hhpbooks.com

The Chronological Guide to Bible Prophecy
Copyright © 2022—Text © Todd Hampson, Artwork © Todd Hampson
Published by Harvest House Publishers
Eugene, Oregon 97408
www.harvesthousepublishers.com

ISBN 978-0-7369-8387-7 (pbk)
ISBN 978-0-7369-8388-4 (eBook)

Library of Congress Control Number: 2022931569

Printed in the United States of America

22 23 24 25 26 27 28 29 30 / VP / 10 9 8 7 6 5 4 3 2 1

Dedicated to Andrew George. Paratrooper, combat veteran, hilarious storyteller, stepbrother, and built-in best friend since first grade. I'm thankful our lives collided early in life. From "Rambo" missions and dirt bikes to rope swing fails and DC subway trips. My childhood would not have been the same without you, and my adult life has been so much richer with you.

Thank you, Lord, for the privilege of writing books about your Word. I get salvation—and all of this too?

To my wife, Tracey, and our grown children. No accomplishment will ever surpass the privilege of loving you and walking through this life together.

To the many scholars cited in this book who have done the careful work of cataloging the compelling details of Bible prophecy.

CONTENTS

Our Fixed Point of Reference

We have this hope as an anchor for the soul, firm and secure.

—HEBREWS 6:19

If you've seen the blockbuster 1995 film *Apollo 13*, you may recall that 56 hours into the United States' third mission to the moon, disaster struck.[1] During a routine cryo stir to check the oxygen levels, an explosion occurred in the tank, causing the loss of one oxygen tank and major damage to the other. The real-life scenario of that event was the genesis of the famous line, "Okay, Houston, we've had a problem here." At that moment, the mission of Apollo 13 changed from landing on the moon to getting back home alive. Against all odds and with the incredible coordinated efforts of the crew and the ground team, everyone aboard Apollo 13 made it home alive.

In the film, there is an extremely tense scene where, after the damaged spacecraft had to abort the mission and slingshot around the moon, a four-minute burn of fuel was needed to shorten the trip by 12 hours. This was necessary because the ship was literally running out of oxygen. By the end of the fuel burn, the module had to be angled correctly in order to make a successful reentry back into the earth's atmosphere. The angle of the entry had to be just right. Too much angle, and the spacecraft would have skipped off the atmosphere into outer space—never to be seen again. Too little angle, and the ship could burst into flames and explode upon entry. To make matters worse, the crew had to conserve electricity, so they were not able to use their computer system. As they initiated the four-minute burn to properly angle the ship, they would have to do so with no assistance from the computer.

In the movie, astronaut Jim Lovell (played by Tom Hanks) looked through a small window that gave him a view of the earth. He surmised that all he needed was a single fixed position in space in order to properly steer the ship during the burst without any assistance from the computer system. If he could keep the earth in the center of the window while they executed the critical four-minute fuel burn, the plan would have a good chance of working. He communicated this to ground command, and they gave him the green light. Lovell then used the visual anchor of the earth in the window to perform the short fuel burn needed to position the ship correctly. The earth had to be centered in the window by the end of the four minutes. If it wasn't, that would mean they were angled incorrectly. This was literally a life-or-death maneuver as they increased the speed of the damaged ship. Fortunately, in their case—after fighting for steering control as the fuel burn began—Lovell was able to get the earth centered in the small window just before the burn ended. Until then, the astronauts, ground team, and millions of people who were following their progress endured an extremely tense few moments with everything on the line.

Apart from God, this world is like a damaged ship floating through time on a collision course with destruction. Fortunately for us, God has given us a fixed point of reference to which we can tether our gaze so that we are not flying blind: his prophetic Word. Prophecy is twofold—it involves *forthtelling* as well as *foretelling*. It is forthtelling in the sense that it instructs its readers how to live rightly with God and man. It is also foretelling, or predictive in nature. In short, the Bible tells us the future, and its declarations have a 100 percent track record of being correct, as confirmed by the hundreds of fulfilled prophecies contained in

PROPHETIC
+RELIABLE
2 PETER 1:19

Scripture. It is this second aspect of prophecy—the foretelling passages (both fulfilled and yet future)—that we will study in this book.

In 2 Peter 1:19, we read, "We...have the prophetic message as something completely reliable, and you will do well to pay attention to it, as to a light shining in a dark place." God's Word is our source of stability in the darkness—and it is inherently prophetic and reliable. These two characteristics go hand in hand.

At its core, the Bible is a *prophetic message* and it is *completely reliable*. Fulfilled prophecy proves Scripture's reliability. The concepts are two sides of the same coin. Fulfilled prophecy is a strong apologetic (defense) that the Bible is from God. The Bible is the only religious book that claims to be the very Word of God and backs up this claim with hundreds of specific fulfilled prophecies. Prophecies are promises. A promise is only as good as the character and ability of the promise-maker.

PROPHECY=PROMISE

We read this bold statement from God in Isaiah 46:9-10: "Remember the former things, those of long ago; I am God, and there is no other; I am God, and there is none like me. I make known the end from the beginning, from ancient times, what is still to come. I say, 'My purpose will stand, and I will do all that I please.'" In a similar manner, Jesus—after telling the disciples some of what was to come—said these words in John 16:4: "I have told you this, so that when their time comes you will remember that I warned you about them."

I'll readily admit that as Christians, we believe some out-of-this-world stuff! We believe in creation and miracles, a global flood and supernatural plagues, the incarnation (where God became man), the resurrection of the dead, the future rapture of the church, a time when God judges the entire world, and the creation of a new heaven and earth. We have not personally witnessed any of those things. So why would we believe they are true?

Experts say that about 26 to 33 percent of the Bible was prophecy at the time it was written. About 75 to 80 percent has already been fulfilled. That is a big down payment that ensures the remaining 20 to 25 percent will in like manner be fulfilled. The single greatest reason we can trust the seemingly insane claims about supernatural events of the past and the miraculous events related to our future is the clear and compelling apologetic of fulfilled Bible prophecy.

Even more compelling is the fact that the 26 to 33 percent of the Bible that is prophetic in nature is not peripheral content—it is inherently connected to the core message of the Bible! If you have read any of my other books, you'll recall that I often refer to prophecy as the central nervous system of the Bible. Biologists study systems in organisms—the digestive system, the cardiovascular system, the muscular system, etc. None of those systems can work without the central nervous system. They are all connected to it and rely on it. Just as humans and animals can't function properly without a healthy central nervous system, the Bible can't be accurately understood without the all-important prophetic passages.

All the key teachings (doctrine/theology), stories, people, and themes in the Bible are somehow connected to Bible prophecy. This is because the Bible (though penned by at least 39 human writers on three different continents over a period of 1,500 years) was inspired by God, who knows everything that is to come. And only God can bring about the perfect fulfillment of every prophecy given in Scripture.

Second Timothy 3:16 tells us that "all Scripture is God-breathed." Second Peter 1:21 tells us that those who wrote prophecy "spoke from God" and were "carried along by the Holy Spirit." In other words, God told them what to write. That is why the whole Bible tells one complete story—a story that is tied together by prophecy and in every way ultimately points to Jesus!

As we chronicle the statistics and the themes of prophecy in the pages of this book, my prayer is that you will be in awe of God, who has given us a compelling and reliable book that point us to his Son and the amazing future promised to each believer who chooses to follow him. I hope you let the concrete statistics and logical facts of prophecy strengthen your faith as a believer in Christ—or break down the walls of skepticism if you are not yet a believer.

I was once a skeptic too, but I could not explain away the undeniable proofs of fulfilled Bible prophecy. That is what led to my salvation, my love of God's Word, and an insatiable desire to plumb its depths—only to find the Bible to be inexhaustible and more beautiful than I ever imagined. I have chronicled some of that for you in the pages of this book. I hope you will enjoy the journey with me!

CHAPTER 1

Why Now?

I believe a book like this is needed for this generation for several reasons. Many have lost a sense of awe and wonder when it comes to the truly incredible feature of prophecy in the Bible. Familiarity can easily lead to complacency. Reconnecting with the Apollo 13 account from the introduction of this book, the first mission to the moon attracted 7 million people to witness the Apollo 11 liftoff. Just a year later, the Apollo 13 liftoff attracted only 200,000. What was once the greatest feat of exploration in history—landing people on the moon—became a routine occurrence that no longer captured the rapt attention of the masses.

The church needs a new moon landing, so to speak. She needs to return to her first love and let the astonishing fact of fulfilled prophecy reinvigorate her passion and excitement for her promised future. Many believers have heard about the amazing truths of prophecy just enough that they have become immune to their intended effect. I pray that this book will reignite a sense of awe and wonder for one of the more compelling features of the Bible (other than Jesus himself), which separates it from every other written work ever produced.

I also believe people are

hungry for something deeper—something that gives answers to the big questions we all want answered. Questions like, Can I really trust the Bible? Is every word of Scripture really from God? I have faith, but where is the compelling evidence that can strengthen my faith in something concrete? There are so many competing voices and there is so much deception in the world right now, so how can I know beyond the shadow of a doubt that I can trust God's Word? Is Jesus really going to return like he said he would? These are the questions on the minds of many. In this book, I want to answer those questions to help strengthen and reignite faith in God's Word through a systematic, chronological guide to Bible prophecy. This book isn't just for prophecy students—it is for every believer!

THE PURPOSES

The main purpose of this book is to catalog prophecy as a biologist would catalog sea creatures, or flowers, or bugs—but in a way that is not overly academic and is fun to read, easy to understand, and practical to study.

I have written several books about Bible prophecy and eschatology, and I have always made an effort to cite reliable sources when I present statistics. But I was compelled to catalog the Bible's prophecies on my own—partly so I could better understand the topic I love so much, but also so I could compare my findings with those of spiritual giants from the recent past.

There are several such studies that have been made over the years. Two frequently cited sources are John Walvoord's book *The Prophecy Knowledge Handbook* and J. Barton Payne's book *The Encyclopedia of Bible Prophecy*. Both books are now out of print, but I was able to find and purchase a copy of each—Walvoord's from 1990 and Payne's from 1973.

To be clear, I did not set out to redo their work, but to see if I came to similar conclusions and to produce a useful resource for a current audience. To my delight and surprise, my conclusions were very similar to those of other scholars who spent a lifetime studying the topic.

Another purpose of this book is to highlight certain prophetic themes that are often overlooked by Christians today. There is much confusion about certain themes that the Bible is actually very clear about. Some of these themes include God's prophetic plan for Israel and the Jewish people; the two advents of the Messiah; the duration, timing, and details of the future tribulation period (known frequently

in the Old Testament as the Day of the Lord); and the timing, nature, and details related to the future kingdom age.

I would venture to say that the vast majority of Christians today focus mostly on the New Testament (understandably so). But without an awareness of the details of the prophecies in the Old Testament, we're left with only part of the picture, and this can lead to some wildly wrong conclusions about prophecy. It does take a bit of work to study and understand the details of the Old Testament prophecies, and one of my goals is to help provide guidance for readers so they can get up to speed quickly. A good understanding of the Old Testament makes the beauty of the New Testament truths shine all the brighter. Viewing the New Testament through the proper framework of the hundreds of detailed prophecies in the Old Testament adds to its richness and clarity.

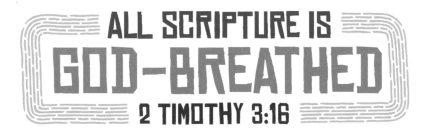

For example, the final book of the Bible—John's book of Revelation—is a thoroughly Jewish book. Revelation has 404 verses, yet contains more than 800 allusions to the Old Testament prophets! There is no way someone can understand Revelation without the context of the Old Testament. One of the key reasons there is so much confusion and fear when it comes to studying Revelation is the context and allusions are not understood. My prayer is that by highlighting some overlooked key themes in the Old Testament, together, we can gain more clarity about the nature of prophecy and end-times events.

THE PROCESS AND CRITERIA

I began cataloging prophecies for this book in September 2019. It took 18 months for me to highlight each prophecy, fulfilled prophecy, and prophetic type in the Bible. Then it took two more months for me to catalog the data and another six months to write and illustrate the book. Needless to say, all of this was a labor of love (and a lot more work than I realized it would be).

In terms of criteria, I was careful to include only clear and specific prophetic content. I considered any statement where God (or a spokesperson for God) foretold something specific that was going to happen in the future. I highlighted all such statements in my Bible from Genesis to Revelation. Then I used the same process for any passage that described the clear fulfillment of previously stated prophecies.

I also highlighted any passages that served as clear typology that prophetically pointed to something in the future (at the time the typology was given). Generally speaking, a *type* is something from the Old Testament that prefigures, or points to, something of greater significance in the New Testament. Most, if not all, typological prophecies relate to the first or second advent of Jesus.

Dr. Roy B. Zuck (who was senior professor/emeritus of the Bible exposition department at Dallas Theological Seminary and the author/editor of more than 70 books) detailed a minimum of five criteria[2] for a biblical type to be valid. I have paraphrased them for you as follows:

1. A notable resemblance between the type and the antitype (the thing it points to)

2. Historical reality of the type and antitype

3. A predictive foreshadowing by the type

4. A heightening (or greater/larger fulfillment) of the antitype

5. Divine design

Zuck added a sixth criteria that he felt was necessary for the type to be an unquestionably valid type. He argued that an Old Testament type must also be designated as such by a passage in the New Testament. Though I think the initial five criteria are likely enough, the added sixth criteria completely removes any possibility of misinterpretation.

For the typology passages mentioned in this book, I generally used all six criteria. Therefore, I did not include certain passages as typology even though I believe they could very well be considered prophetic typology (including, for example, several passages in the Song of Solomon that could be seen as pointing to Christ and the church). I chose to take the most conservative approach in an attempt to convince even the most skeptical of readers that fulfilled Bible prophecy is a compelling proof of the divine origin of the Scriptures.

Once I physically highlighted each prophecy, fulfilled prophecy, and prophetic type, I went chapter by chapter to chronicle the number of verses for each. Next, I put all of this information into a spreadsheet and totaled up the numbers book by book (truth be known, I hired my son Luke to do most of the spreadsheet work). Finally, I worked out the percentages, then laid the findings out in the charts you'll see at the beginning of each book of the Bible.

THE BOTTOM LINE

I intentionally took a very conservative approach toward cataloging Bible prophecies. I only included verses that contained specific prophetic details. In many cases, I could have also included some of the setup or surrounding verses for context, but I chose to use only verses that specifically contain prophetic details that either predict the future or show how a previous prophecy was fulfilled. There were also several instances where I could have cited more of what is very likely prophetic typology. Therefore, the statistical conclusions I arrived at are most likely lower than the actual percentage of prophetic content in the Bible. Please keep that in mind as you view the charts for each book of the Bible and as you compare these statistics with those of other authors and theologians who have come before me.

Through much study and a lifetime of teaching, great theologians such as Dr. John F. Walvoord, Dr. J. Dwight Pentecost, and Dr. J. Barton Payne (along with other theologians) have left a legacy of scholarship and reliable resources. In no way is this book meant to replace their works. Rather, I felt a current resource—written and illustrated in a way that makes the content extremely accessible—would be well received at this time in history when new generations of Christians are waking up to the compelling and relevant truths of Bible prophecy and eschatology. The increasing instability of today's world is causing many to take a fresh look at the prophetic claims of Scripture. This book is intended to equip these people in a simple and compelling fashion.

As I noted above, I also took the conservative approach with skeptics in mind. In other words, I went out of my way to be sure I cataloged the clearest and most compelling examples of prophetic content in the Bible. In the following chapters, you'll note the estimated percentage of prophetic content found in each book of the Bible. When you total everything up, here's the bottom line of my very conservative findings:

At least 26 percent of the Bible (8,067 verses) is prophecy. Of that total, 25 percent (2,037 verses) is yet-future/end-times prophecy. The numbers break down as follows:

> 31,103 total Bible verses (23,145 Old Testament;
> 7,958 New Testament)
>
> 8,067 total prophetic content (26 percent)
>
> 2,037 yet future (7 percent of the Bible and 25 percent
> of total prophetic content)

Again, these are conservative numbers. I am certain there are quite a few additional passages or typologies that I could have included as prophetic content. There were also many verses I could have included where the text was reminding the reader of fulfilled prophecy. For example, there were many times when God is referred to as the God who rescued his people from the land of Egypt. Even though the exodus was a fulfillment of prophecy, I only included the actual event of the exodus as fulfilled prophecy. All of that to say, I consider the stats above to be a raw and stripped-down baseline consisting strictly of clear, bona fide Bible prophecies.

When describing the amount of prophecy found in Scripture, I believe it is okay to cite a range of percentages because analyzing prophetic passages is not an exact science and there have been many credible scholars who have taken on this momentous task. That is why I would recommend framing the percentages as I did in the introduction. I've included that information again here. I believe a good general way to cite the amount of prophecy in the Bible is as follows:

Experts cite that the Bible is made up of 26 to 33 percent prophecy. About 75 to 80 percent has already been fulfilled, leaving the remaining 20 to 25 percent for yet-future end-times events.

THE INTERPRETATION METHODS

There are four main interpretation methods that people have used to study prophecy. I don't have the space to go into lengthy detail on each, but here is a brief overview of the four methods and an explanation of why I believe the futurist approach is the single correct method Christians should use to interpret Bible prophecy.

The Idealist View: Prophecy Is Allegory

This view is also sometimes referred to as the spiritual view. This is because it allegorizes or spiritualizes prophetic texts, particularly with regard to the book of Revelation. This school of thought arose around AD 190 from the area of Alexandria, Egypt, and was adopted by the fifth-century theologian Augustine of Hippo, then promoted by the official church until after the Reformation. While other interpretation methods existed, the Roman Catholic Church stifled any dissent during that time. Augustine's teaching became the dominant view for centuries and carried over into the Protestant Reformation era led by Martin Luther and John Calvin.

The main problem with this method of interpretation is that when we allegorize certain prophetic sections of Scripture, we open ourselves to the risk of making a passage say something it doesn't intend to say. The interpreter becomes the standard instead of Scripture itself. This has led people to come up with wildly varying meanings for specific prophetic texts and leaves us with little confidence that certain passages can truly be understood.

The Preterist View: The Prophecies Already Happened

The basic claim of this view is that Bible prophecy is actually Bible history. The preterist view puts forth the notion that the book of Revelation presents a symbolic picture of first-century events rather than future events that will occur at the end of our current age.

Within this view there are two lines of thought. Certain teachers assert that some of the book of Revelation has already occurred (partial preterism), while others teach that all of it has (full preterism)—namely in AD 70, when the Romans destroyed Jerusalem.

The main problems with this view are that evidence indicates John wrote the book of Revelation around AD 95 while exiled on the Island of Patmos, about 15 years after the fall of Jerusalem. Also, we know for certain that the major judgments described in Revelation and the physical return of Christ to earth did not occur in AD 70. There are too many prophetic details in Revelation that clearly did not take place in AD 70.

The Historicist View: Prophecy Is Merely an Overview of History

This view first appeared around AD 300 and attempts to interpret Revelation simply as a symbolic representation of history of all that has taken place and will take place in church history from John's time to the end. This view was popular during the Reformation era but has many problems, and there are as many as 50 versions of this view.

This view also allegorizes Scripture, and each generation of its adopters have changed the meaning of allegorized symbols based on the events, rulers, and conditions of their day. In other words, the way Bible prophecy is interpreted constantly changes, leaving us uncertain as to what the Bible really is saying. This is the weakest of the four views, and it has few adherents in our day.

The Futurist View: Prophecy Understood Literally

This view teaches that the end-times prophetic events described in Revelation are yet future. It holds that these events and related passages in the Old Testament will occur literally in the future and are to be understood by the plain sense of the text. The book of Revelation clearly claims to be prophecy, and prophecy, by nature, has a future fulfillment.

The hundreds of prophecies in the Bible that have already been fulfilled were fulfilled literally, not figuratively. There is no indication anywhere in Scripture that God suggests we switch to a new method of understanding prophecy. A prophecy is given, then at a later time it is fulfilled, just as described. That is the clear nature and pattern of prophecy.

The futurist view is the only one that interprets Revelation literally—which is the same way we interpret the rest of Scripture. In the passages where we find symbols, the answers are provided in the immediate or broader context of Scripture, and not from our own ideas. Where figures of speech are used, they are clear figures of speech that were understood by the original audience. The futurist view makes the most logical sense, honors God as a clear communicator, uses the same method to interpret all of Scripture consistently, and takes God's Word at face value.

IDEALIST PROPHECY IS ALLEGORY

PRETERIST THE PROPHECIES ALREADY HAPPENED

HISTORICIST PROPHECY IS MERELY AN OVERVIEW OF HISTORY

FUTURIST PROPHECY IS UNDERSTOOD LITERALLY

The book of Revelation describes unprecedented supernatural events. Rather than explain them away because they are too hard to believe, we should take God at his word. I've heard prophecy experts state that the book of Revelation is not hard to understand—it's just hard to believe. If we believe Genesis 1:1 truly happened, we should have no problem believing every detail in the book of Revelation will come to pass, just as all earlier Bible prophecies have come to pass.

The idealist, preterist, and historicist views all allegorize or spiritualize Scripture in some fashion. Ultimately, by opening the door to allegorical interpretation, these views let the reader come up with interpretations that may stray from what the apostle John intended to communicate in Revelation.

The futurist view is the only approach that pursues a consistent literal understanding of Scripture from beginning to end. Ultimately, then, there are two main categories of interpretive thought: an allegorical approach to interpreting Scripture, or a literal approach to interpreting Scripture. For the reasons I stated earlier, I am firmly convinced we are to interpret Scripture literally, and that when it comes to understanding Bible prophecy, the futurist view is the one that makes the greatest sense.

Either Scripture can be spiritualized, with the interpreter deciding which passages have symbolic meaning, or all of Scripture is meant to be taken literally and understood by the plain and clear meanings of the words themselves.

With the help of all this background information, let's dive in and explore the prophecies of the Bible!

CHAPTER 2

Jam-Packed Genesis

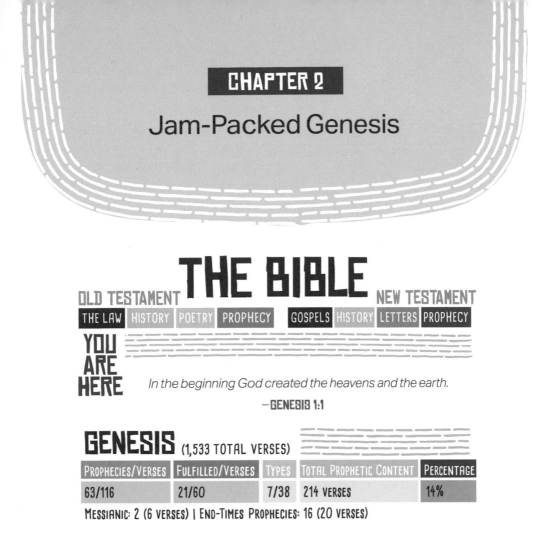

THE BIBLE

OLD TESTAMENT | NEW TESTAMENT

| THE LAW | HISTORY | POETRY | PROPHECY | GOSPELS | HISTORY | LETTERS | PROPHECY |

YOU ARE HERE

In the beginning God created the heavens and the earth.
—GENESIS 1:1

GENESIS (1,533 TOTAL VERSES)

PROPHECIES/VERSES	FULFILLED/VERSES	TYPES	TOTAL PROPHETIC CONTENT	PERCENTAGE
63/116	21/60	7/38	214 VERSES	14%

MESSIANIC: 2 (6 VERSES) | END-TIMES PROPHECIES: 16 (20 VERSES)

In Hebrew, the first verse of Genesis contains just seven words. In the early chapters of Genesis, God establishes a seven-day week, providing the basis for our modern-day seven-day week. This foundational number becomes the number that represents *completion* throughout the pages of Scripture. Humans are built for seven-day weeks. Throughout history, various attempts have been made to modify this, but regardless of culture, geography, or time period, people have universally measured time in terms of a seven-day week. This is by design.

This is but one of hundreds of critical cornerstone details established in jam-packed Genesis. Foundational details from the book of Genesis establish

the precedent for the Bible and how its truths play out in real life. And the bedrock prophetic themes established in Genesis are progressively unveiled to us throughout the pages of Scripture.

According to Jewish tradition, Genesis (along with the remaining four books of the Torah) was written by Moses. And 2 Peter 1:21 tells us that all writers of the Bible were "carried along by the Holy Spirit" as they wrote.

Above all, you must understand that no prophecy of Scripture came about by the prophet's own interpretation of things. For prophecy never had its origin in the human will, but prophets, though human, spoke from God as they were carried along by the Holy Spirit (verses 20-21).

Genesis is jam-packed with foundational prophecies and prophetic types that establish the key themes for the rest of the Bible. It is the root system from which the rest of Scripture grows.

Genesis is the book of beginnings in every sense. It is the essential bedrock of the Word of God. It informs us about the beginning of time, space, matter, life, sin, salvation, humans, and God's chosen people through whom the Messiah would come. It provides foundational details about creation, the fall, the flood, the dispersion of the nations, and key figures including Abraham, Isaac, Jacob, and Joseph.

Jam-packed Genesis pours the concrete that the rest of the Bible is built upon. No wonder the book has been so attacked, maligned, and sidelined over the past few generations. The enemies of God have attempted to destroy the foundation of the Bible through naturalist philosophies, higher criticism, secular humanist ideology, and liberal theology—all of which attempt to undermine the fact that Scripture is trustworthy and true. Yet it stands.

Archeology, history, and prophecy all provide evidence that supports this foundational book's veracity, accuracy, and longevity. Fulfilled prophecy is one of the strongest proofs of the Bible's divine origin—and Genesis serves as a vanguard.

KEY PROPHETIC DETAILS IN GENESIS

There are no prophecies in the first chapter of Genesis, but what we do find is the precedent of God speaking things into existence. God created the universe *ex nihilo* (out of nothing). This establishes the fact that when God speaks or proclaims something, it will inevitably come to pass. God spoke the universe into existence. Similarly, he would also come to speak about future events that were guaranteed to occur just as foretold. God is outside of time, and he alone can tell history in advance.

(SEE GENESIS 1:3, 6-7, 9, 11, 14-15, 20-21, 24, 26-27)

The first clear prophecy in Scripture is Genesis 2:17, which reads, "You must not eat from the tree of the knowledge of good and evil, for when you eat from it you will certainly die." While this prophecy may not be as compelling to a skeptic as something that can be externally verified in history (such as the prophecy of successive Gentile empires in Daniel chapter 2, or the many prophecies about Israel becoming a nation again), it is indeed the first prophecy in the Bible.

The Protoevangelium

Speaking of firsts, we also find the first prophecy of the future Messiah in chapter 3 of Genesis. Genesis 3:15 provides the first glimpse of Jesus—seen here as the "offspring" of the woman. This passage, known in theological circles as the protoevangelium, is the first (Greek, *proto*) prophecy of the good news (Greek, *evangelion*) of the future Messiah.

Genesis 3:15 provided minimal information—merely that this future offspring would be virgin-born (offspring of the woman) and that he would crush the head of the serpent (whom we learn definitively in Revelation 12

is Satan), though he (the offspring of the woman) would be wounded in the process (a veiled reference to the crucifixion of Christ).

As with other "firsts" in the first book of the Bible, this key verse serves as the bedrock upon which future prophecies would be progressively revealed. In my book *The Non-Prophet's Guide™ to Spiritual Warfare*, I highlight in detail how this prophecy began a deadly game of cosmic chess as Satan adjusted his warfare tactics based on each additional detail God would provide about this future offspring of the woman.

The Gospel Hidden in Plain Sight

The Bible is an amazing book. The more we study it, the more we realize its depth. It is God's eternal and inexhaustible Word (Isaiah 40:8; 1 Peter 1:23). The plain language of prophecy is quite compelling, but there are also additional layers of meaning we discover when we look into the original languages

THE GOSPEL REVEALED IN NAMES IN GENESIS 5

ADAM	man [is]
SETH	appointed
ENOSH	mortal
KENAN	sorrow [but]
MAHALALEL	the blessed God
JARED	shall come down
ENOCH	teaching
METHUSELAH	his death shall bring
LAMECH	the despairing
NOAH	comfort/rest

and the specific meanings of words and names. For example, in Genesis chapter 5, a study of the names given in what would appear to most as merely a boring genealogical record is actually a profound prophetic layout of the core theme of the entire Bible.

When the meaning of the Hebrew names from the genealogy are strung together, they form a sentence that essentially says, "Man is appointed mortal sorrow, but the blessed God will come down teaching and his death will bring the despairing rest."

Also, the taking up of Enoch to heaven serves as a type of the rapture before judgment (verse 24—"God took him"). And it has been observed that the meaning of Methuselah's name—"his death shall bring"—served to warn that at his death, judgment would occur. Indeed, after Methuselah died, the flood came.

Typology

Yet another first in Genesis is the establishment of typology. Biblical typology establishes the idea that a literal, historical narrative can serve as a type or template of how God will bring about a greater future component of the biblical narrative. We see this in modern storytelling. For example, a well-crafted movie will foreshadow key plot points via typology that shows up early in the film through subtle symbolism, clear archetypes, or otherwise introducing themes on a basic level.

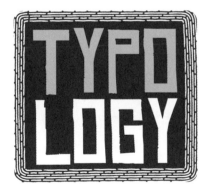

In the book of Genesis, we see the first key typological elements in Scripture. Both the flood in Genesis 6 and the destruction of Sodom and Gomorrah in chapter 19 establish a pattern of God's judgment that will unfold on a much broader scale during the end times with events surrounding the return of Christ as foretold in the Bible's final book—Revelation.

In both the flood and the destruction of Sodom and Gomorrah, we find this pattern: God warns of coming judgment; he waits as long as he can until wickedness has reached its peak; he removes the righteous; his wrath falls on those who remain. While there are differing views about the order of events related to the future tribulation period, there are key prophecy scholars who agree that this early prophetic typology in Genesis begins to establish support for the view that God will remove the righteous (via the rapture) prior to his wrath falling on the entire world during the seven-year tribulation. I'll share much more about this in chapter 14 of this book, where I will present the various views of the timing of the rapture along with a word about the need for unity in the body of Christ when believers disagree on their eschatological viewpoints. Ultimately, there is only one correct view, but this is not an issue that Christians should divide over.

The Tower of Babel

In Genesis chapter 11, we bump into another early prototype of a greater future event. The account about the Tower of Babel describes the first attempt at a global government establishing itself with the latest technology in open rebellion against God. This event foreshadows the future tribulation period when a figure commonly known as the antichrist will rise to power and—

with initial help of the false prophet and a global governing body—rule the world for a horrific seven-year period (see Daniel 9:27; Matthew 24:15; Revelation 6:2; 13:1-10).

Father Abraham

Another important line of biblical prophecy that begins in Genesis is the call of the patriarch Abraham in Genesis 12 and the chapters that follow. Additional prophetic details are provided and affirmed as the Abrahamic promise is reiterated to his son Isaac and grandson Jacob (Israel). The call of Abraham in chapter 12 contains the foundational prophecies establishing the people of the then-future nation of Israel (Jacob's eventual new name) as God's chosen people, through whom the Messiah would come.

There are in fact five specific covenants that God made with the Jewish people—all but one of which are permanent and unconditional promises to them. I list the covenants here so you'll have them in mind as you study this book and see these key prophetic themes emerge as we make our way through the Bible.

1. *The Abrahamic covenant* (Genesis 12:1-7; 13:14-17; 15:1-21; 17:1-14; 22:15-18) Characteristics: unconditional and permanent (covered in some detail below)

2. *The Mosaic covenant* (Exodus 19–24; Leviticus 26*; Deuteronomy 28*) Characteristics: conditional/temporal and prophetic (*blessings for obedience and curses for disobedience, all of which Israel experienced)

3. *The Davidic covenant* (2 Samuel 7:16; 1 Chronicles 17:10-14) Characteristics: unconditional, prophetic, and permanent (will be fulfilled in the future millennial kingdom)

4. *The land covenant* (Deuteronomy 29:1–30:20) Characteristics: unconditional, prophetic, and permanent (the people of Israel regathered from the nations, placed back in their land as one prosperous nation)

5. *The new covenant* (Jeremiah 31:31-34; Romans 11:26) Characteristics: unconditional, prophetic, and permanent

Note: There are a total of eight covenants, including three others God made with all of mankind. They are the Edenic covenant (Genesis 1:28-30; 2:15-17; Hosea 6:7), the Adamic covenant (Genesis 3:14-19), and the Noahic covenant (Genesis 9:1-17). The Edenic covenant was conditional/temporary, while the other two are permanent/eternal.

The covenants with the Jewish people all started with the Abrahamic covenant found in the book of Genesis. Here are some key verses to consider; these are foundational to other prophecies that I'll point out in the prophets and the Psalms as they relate specifically to the Jewish people and the nation of Israel—both in history and in yet-future prophecies related to the events of the end times.

Space does not allow for me to include all the verses in Genesis chapters 12–18 related to the Abrahamic covenant. Instead, I have listed a few key verses below. As you read them, please notice a few important (and commonly overlooked) details, including the core, permanent, unconditional, and yet-future nature of the full promise. These details are vital to remember as we study other prophecies related to God's program for the Jewish people in our current era and in key future end-time events.

Core

Here's the initial covenant God made with Abraham (at the time still named Abram). In Genesis 12:1-3, we read,

> The Lord had said to Abram, "Go from your country, your people and your father's household to the land I will show you. I will make you into a great nation, and I will bless you; I will make your name great, and you will be a blessing. I will bless those who bless you, and whoever curses you I will curse; and all peoples on earth will be blessed through you."

Permanent

Additional details are provided in Genesis 13:14-15, where we read, "The Lord said to Abram after Lot had parted from him, 'Look around from where you are, to the north and south, to the east and west. All the land that you see I will give to you and your offspring *forever*.'"

Unconditional

In chapter 15, the promise is confirmed by the cutting of a covenant, an ancient practice where both parties would confirm an agreement by cutting a sacrificial animal in half and walking in between the separated pieces. In verses 12 and 17, we read, "As the sun was setting, Abram fell into a deep sleep, and a thick and dreadful darkness came over him...When the sun had set and darkness had fallen, a smoking firepot with a blazing torch appeared and passed between the pieces."

Notice that Abram (who would later become Abraham) was asleep when God completed the covenant. This was a one-way covenant. The Lord himself walked through the separated pieces of the sacrifice—essentially saying,

"If I break this covenant, may I be cut in pieces like this sacrifice." This was a common custom of the day, but usually both parties would walk between the pieces. Here, only God walked through while Abraham was sleeping. This is no small detail.

Yet Future

In terms of fulfilled prophecy, God did make Abraham into a great nation. God blessed Abraham, made his name great, and blessed the entire world through him (through the Messiah and the Bible). But there are some aspects of the Abrahamic covenant that have yet to be fulfilled. In Genesis 15:18, we read, "On that day the LORD made a covenant with Abram and said, 'To your descendants I give this land, from the Wadi of Egypt to the great river, the Euphrates.'"

As of today, Israel—in its ancient and modern forms—has never occupied all the land from the Nile to the Euphrates. The complete fulfillment of this prophecy will occur during the future millennial kingdom. Up to this time, all fulfilled prophecies have come to pass literally. There is no legitimate reason to say that still-future prophecies will not also be similarly fulfilled. God's track record is 100 percent accuracy—even when it has seemed impossible for a prophecy to be fulfilled.

The Prophetic Lamb

In Genesis 22, when God instructs Abraham to sacrifice his son Isaac as a means of testing Abraham's faith, there is a curious prophetic detail that is easily overlooked. In verse 7, Isaac asks the logical question, "Where is the lamb for the burnt offering?" Abraham replies, "God

himself will provide the lamb" (verse 8). Later, after the Angel of the Lord (the preincarnate Jesus) halts the action (verse 12) and highlights the fact that Isaac was Abraham's "only son," the text tells us there was a ram caught in the bushes, which Abraham then used as the burnt offering.

Here's the powerful prophetic import: Abraham said God would provide a lamb, but in the narrative described above, God provided a ram. In other words, Abraham's proclamation that God would provide a lamb was pointing to a greater future sacrifice. The New Testament records that Jesus was "the Lamb of God who takes away the sin of the world!" (John 1:29). We also discover that Jesus was crucified on Passover (when lambs were sacrificed) and hung on the cross at the same time of the day when lambs were being sacrificed on the Jewish holiday. Even more compelling is the fact that, as most theologians believe, the Angel of the Lord in Genesis 22 was the preincarnate Jesus. If that were not enough, we discover through a careful study of Scripture that the place where Abraham ascended to sacrifice his son was the same area where, roughly 2,000 years later, God the Father would sacrifice his only Son on the cross at Golgotha!

Joseph as a Type of Jesus

As we read the lengthy story of Joseph found in Genesis chapters 37–42, it is easy to overlook the typology. But upon careful observation, we find several parallels between the narrative of Joseph and the life of Christ. Indeed, an

entire chapter could be dedicated solely to this compelling typology, but for our purposes here, I've distilled some of the key typological details below. (Also worthy of note is the fact that Genesis 40 marks the first appearance, in the Bible, of a prophetic dream and interpretation.)

Here is a comparison of several details demonstrating the typology of Jesus found in the story of Joseph. It's a long (yet incomplete) list, but well worth the time to observe the comparisons.

Joseph was especially loved by his father (Genesis 37:3).
God said of Jesus, "This is my Son, whom I love" (Matthew 3:17).

Joseph was one of the sons of Israel (Jacob).
Jesus was a son of Israel (that is, from the Jewish nation of Israel).

Joseph's brothers did not accept him; they hated him (Genesis 37:4-5). The Jewish leaders did not accept Christ (Matthew 21:45-46), but hated him (Mark 12:12; John 15:24).

Joseph's brothers rejected his right to rule (Genesis 37:8). The Jewish leaders rejected Jesus's right to rule (Luke 19:14).

Joseph's brothers conspired against him (Genesis 37:23). The Jewish religious leaders conspired against Jesus (Matthew 27:1; Mark 12:12).

Joseph was stripped of his garments (Genesis 37:23). Jesus was stripped of his garments (Matthew 27:28).

Joseph was sold for silver (Genesis 37:28). Jesus was sold for silver (Matthew 26:15).

Everything Joseph put his hand to prospered (Genesis 39:3). God's favor was on Jesus during his three-and-a-half-year ministry (Isaiah 53:10; Matthew 3:17).

The Pharaoh gave Joseph authority over all things (Genesis 39:4-8). All authority in heaven and earth was given to Jesus (Matthew 28:18; John 3:35).

Joseph's own brothers did not recognize him (Genesis 42:8). The Jewish leaders and most of the people did not recognize their Messiah (Matthew 16:3; Mark 15:13; Luke 12:56).

Joseph was repeatedly tempted and did not sin (Genesis 39:9). Jesus was tempted in all things yet was without sin (Luke 4:1-13; Hebrews 4:15).

Joseph was bound (Genesis 39:20). Jesus was bound (Matthew 27:2).

Joseph was condemned with two criminals (Genesis 40:2-3). Jesus was crucified with two criminals (Luke 23:32).

One criminal was restored and the other was killed (Genesis 40:21-22). One criminal joined Jesus in paradise and the other did not (Luke 23:43).

The criminals Joseph was with were a cupbearer and a bread baker (Genesis 40:2).
Jesus initiated communion with wine and bread (Luke 22:17-19).

Joseph was trustworthy and wise (Genesis 41:39).
Jesus finished his work completely with full integrity and wisdom (Mark 1:11, 27; Luke 2:49; John 19:28-30).

Joseph's brothers bowed their knee to him (Genesis 42:6).
"At the name of Jesus every knee should bow" (Philippians 2:10).
All remaining Jewish people will one day recognize their Messiah (Zechariah 12:10; Matthew 23:39; John 19:37; Romans 11:26).

God sovereignly planned the suffering of Joseph in advance to save many (Genesis 50:20).
Jesus's suffering was sovereignly planned to save all who would believe in him (John 3:16; Revelation 13:8).

Joseph was made ruler over all of Egypt (Genesis 41:42-44).
Jesus will one day rule the entire world (Isaiah 9:6; Matthew 28:18; Revelation 20:4).

Joseph married a foreign bride (Genesis 41:45).
The church is the bride of Christ, and we are "joint heirs" with him in his glory (John 3:29; Romans 8:17).

Joseph was imprisoned based on false charges (Genesis 39:19-20).
During the trials of Jesus, many false witnesses testified against him (Mark 14:56).

As the seven-year famine progressed in Egypt, Joseph revealed himself to his brothers (Genesis 45:1-5).
During the future seven-year tribulation, God's main focus will be to reveal himself to the Jewish people (Daniel 9:26-27; Zechariah 12:10; Romans 11:26, 29; Revelation 7:4; 12:5-6).

After revealing himself to his brothers, Joseph gained all the land for Pharaoh (Genesis 47:20).
During the tribulation period, Jesus will reveal himself to the Jewish people and reclaim the entire earth (Revelation 5:5; 11:15).

Joseph's brothers later repented for what they did to him
(Genesis 50:15-18).
The Jewish people who survive the tribulation period will repent and
turn to Christ (Zechariah 12:10; Matthew 23:39; Romans 11:26).

THE PROPHETIC CRESCENDO OF GENESIS

In the second to last chapter of Genesis, we find the account of Jacob
(Israel) prophetically blessing each of his sons. Some of the blessings sound
more like curses, and the entire chapter reads more like a prophecy than what
you and I would typically think of as a blessing. These are Jacob's all-important
last words to his children, laid out in prophetic prose.

While the NIV Bible renders Genesis 49:1 as "Jacob called for his sons and
said: 'Gather around so I can tell you what will happen to you in days to
come,'" the literal Hebrew translation reads "in the last days" instead of "in
days to come."

So, Jacob is speaking prophetically to each tribe of Israel about their future
trajectory all the way to the end. While the entire chapter is worthy of study,
there is one section I would like to highlight due to its messianic significance—
Jacob's prophetic blessings to Judah (through whom the Messiah would come).

As you read this section of Genesis 49, keep in mind that Jesus is referred to as the "Lion of the tribe of Judah" (Revelation 5:5) who will protect and save the remnant of Jewish people at the end of the future tribulation period (Zechariah 12:10; Matthew 23:39; Romans 11:26; Revelation 12:15-17), destroy the antichrist and his armies (Revelation 19:11-21), then set up his millennial kingdom for 1,000 years on earth, during which he will reign. Many details about Jesus's advents find connection points to this passage.

In Genesis 49:8-12, we read,

> Judah, your brothers will praise you; your hand will be on the neck of your enemies; your father's sons will bow down to you. You are a lion's cub, Judah; you return from the prey, my son. Like a lion he crouches and lies down, like a lioness—who dares to rouse him? The scepter will not depart from Judah, nor the ruler's staff from between his feet, until he to whom it belongs shall come and the obedience of the nations shall be his. He will tether his donkey to a vine, his colt to the choicest branch; he will wash his garments in wine, his robes in the blood of grapes. His eyes will be darker than wine, his teeth whiter than milk.

Here we see the conquering and ruling messianic prophetic details about Judah. All of these and more give us key prophetic insights into the Messiah at his first coming as well as during his future reign in the millennial kingdom.

THE CRITICAL LINK: ORIGINS AND LAST THINGS

As you can see, the study of first things is of utmost importance in Scripture. Much like the opening pages of a novel or the first few minutes of a good film, fundamental information is contained in the inceptive section of any great work. This is definitely true about the first book of the Bible, which explains our origins, the problem that needed a remedy, the promise of a future Savior, and other foundational truths that undergird the rest of the Bible. The prophecies and prophetic types set forth in the Bible's lead-off book set the precedent for the rest of Scripture. In the ensuing trajectory, prophetic details, themes, and types are progressively built up on this all-important foundational text that we call Genesis.

It is no wonder that well-crafted subversions from the enemy have come first and foremost to the books of Genesis and Revelation. No two books have been attacked or neglected more than these bookends of Scripture. Naturalists and liberal theologians have sought to undermine the authenticity and reliability of Genesis for the past 250 years. The enemy would like nothing more than to divert our attention away from foundational truths. Once this critical foundation is cracked in the hearts and minds of people, the rest of the structure is ignored or greatly misunderstood. On the other end of the biblical spectrum, the book of Revelation is often seen as confusing at best—and utterly unknowable or irrelevant at worst. We shouldn't be surprised that both Genesis and Revelation are under attack these days, just as we are nearing the end of the age.

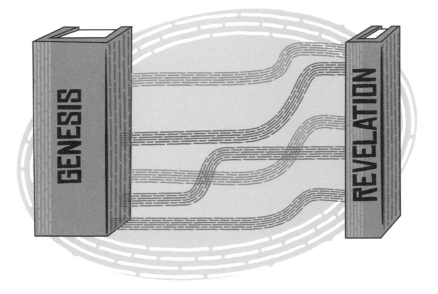

There is a critical prophetic link between these two key books, and the enemy has done his best to keep people disinterested or preoccupied so they miss the all-important truths found within them. In Genesis, we discover our roots, and in Revelation, we learn about our eternal future. Every key theme and theological truth finds its origin in Genesis and its ultimate culmination in Revelation. And remarkably, everything is connected together through the eternal glue of Bible prophecy. The Bible is a "book of books" that begins with eternity past and ends with eternity future. The core questions that people have about their origins and their future are answered by Genesis and Revelation—and everything is meticulously woven together by the other 64 books between them.

The foundational truths of God's prophetic Word are established in the jam-packed book of Genesis. That's why it's so important for us to be familiar with it.

CHAPTER 3

The Rest of the Torah

The LORD said to him, "Know for certain that for four hundred years your descendants will be strangers in a country not their own and that they will be enslaved and mistreated there. But I will punish the nation they serve as slaves, and afterward they will come out with great possessions. You, however, will go to your ancestors in peace and be buried at a good old age. In the fourth generation your descendants will come back here, for the sin of the Amorites has not yet reached its full measure."

—GENESIS 15:13–16

I'm an animation producer by trade, so I often think in terms of development, narrative, visuals, character development, and story arcs. My family jokes that I can't watch animated shows or films like a normal person. I view them through the eyes of a story developer or animation producer. Along this line of thinking, when it comes to the Torah, I view Genesis as the pilot episode and the remaining four books as subsequent episodes—and the subsequent sections of the Bible as additional seasons. They are all part of the same overall narrative, but each book builds out each season (section of Scripture) and each season builds out the entire series (the Bible). With each flip of the page or unfurling of the scroll, the story moves forward—building tension and adding more practical theological information.

In pilot episodes, the main purpose is to introduce all the key characters, themes, and conflicts. Another purpose is to introduce the "world" of the show—the rules of the environment in which the entire story will take place. Genesis does all of this and more—complete with hints of what to expect in future episodes (via prophecy, prophetic types, and vital hints of what to watch for).

With the critical information learned from the pilot episode, fans watch the rest of the season with great anticipation as to how the main storyline and the individual character story arcs will unfold. I often use analogies that people are familiar with because they help us to see why systematic Bible study is so important. People rarely watch a season finale without any knowledge of the series. Similarly, people rarely have much interest in the book of Revelation if they are not already riveted by the initial storyline and progressively revealed early episodes.

While I do acknowledge there is value in topical studies, in my opinion, there is no better tool for discipleship and grasping God's Word than a systematic study of Scripture. In this model, the proverbial pilot episode (Genesis) and the early episodes that build upon it (the next four books of the Jewish Torah) are absolutely foundational to a healthy and accurate understanding of the rest of the Bible.

From as far back as we can ascertain, Jewish tradition holds that Moses was the author of the Torah (the first five books of the Old Testament). Moses is the key figure in the book of Exodus, the recorder of the Law in Leviticus, the historian in the book of Numbers, and the prophetic prognosticator for the Promised Land in Deuteronomy.

Using our analogy from above, Genesis serves as the pilot episode that sets the stage for the entire show, and the rest of the Torah completes season one, which ends with the mysterious death of Moses and a nail-biting cliffhanger with his successor, Joshua, poised to lead God's people into the Promised Land. Woven throughout the narrative are specific prophecies that provide clarifying details of what is to come.

EXODUS

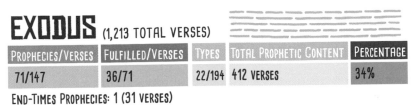

EXODUS (1,213 TOTAL VERSES)

PROPHECIES/VERSES	FULFILLED/VERSES	TYPES	TOTAL PROPHETIC CONTENT	PERCENTAGE
71/147	36/71	22/194	412 VERSES	34%

END-TIMES PROPHECIES: 1 (31 VERSES)

I'll open this section on Exodus with a prophecy from the book of Genesis. In one of the many prophecies related to the Abrahamic covenant, we learn of a key prophetic detail directly related to the book of Exodus. In Genesis 15, we read about how the Abrahamic promise was to unfold. Here's the paraphrase: "Abe, you are going to have a ton of descendants, but first they'll be stuck in a foreign land for 400 years, waiting for the right time to take the land that I'm giving to them."

The book of Exodus documents the fulfillment of this prophecy. It is interesting to see how prophecies will provide us with the basic picture of what is to come—the broad-brush strokes. But the fulfillments of prophecies unfold with many additional details. This is usually the case with prophecy and is good to keep in mind as we study eschatology (the study of last things) and the events surrounding the return of Christ. Scripture provides us with the big-picture information, but we don't usually know all of the smaller setup details that must take place. More on this as we study the prophets and the book of Revelation later in this book! With that brief overview, let's take a look at some of the notable prophetic sections from the book of Exodus.

The Typology of the Plagues

Many people find it interesting that the plagues leading up to the exodus show up in a broader form during the future tribulation period. A careful study of the 21 judgments described in the book of Revelation reveal a prophetic pattern that hearkens back to the plagues in the book of Exodus. See the chart on the next page for the comparisons.

PROPHETIC FORESHADOWS OF
THE PLAGUES

	PLAGUE	EGYPT	TRIBULATION
1	WATER TO BLOOD	Ex. 7:20; Ps. 105:29	Rev. 8:8-9; Rev. 11:6; Rev. 16:3-6
2	FROGS	Ex. 8:6; Ps. 105:30	Rev. 16:13-14
3	LICE	Ex. 8:24; Ps. 105:31	Rev. 11:6+?
4	FLIES	Ex. 8:24; Ps. 105:31	Rev. 11:6+?
5	LIVESTOCK KILLED	Ex. 9:6	Rev. 8:9+?
6	BOILS	Ex. 9:10	Rev. 16:2
7	HAIL	Ex. 9:23; Ps. 105:32	Rev. 8:7; Rev. 16:21
8	LOCUSTS	Ex. 10:13; Ps. 105:34	Rev. 9:3-11
9	DARKNESS	Ex. 10:22	Rev. 8:12; Rev. 9:2; Rev. 16:10
10	DEATH OF 1ST-BORN	Ex. 12:29; Ps. 105:36	Rev. 13:3?

The Prophetic Precedent of Passover

You may recall that in the New Testament Gospel accounts, Jesus was crucified on Passover. This was not random or coincidental. The very first Passover—found here in Exodus chapter 12—was a detailed prophetic foreshadow of the events surrounding the crucifixion of Jesus. If you'll recall from our discussion in the last chapter, Jesus is depicted as the Lamb of God in the New Testament (see John 1:29; Revelation 12:11) and was literally inspected (went on trial) and sacrificed (sentenced to crucifixion) on Passover (John 19:14, 16). Here

is a brief comparison showing some of the details of the first Passover and how they pointed to the future Messiah:

The sacrifice was to be a lamb (Exodus 12:3, 5).
Jesus is known as the Lamb of God.

The sacrifice was to be a male (Exodus 12:5).
Jesus is a male.

The sacrifice was to be without blemish (Exodus 12:5).
Jesus is the sinless Son of God (2 Corinthians 5:21).

The sacrifice was to be in the prime of life (Exodus 12:5).
Jesus was about 33 when he was crucified.

The sacrifice was to be presented and examined days before Passover (Exodus 12:3-6).
Jesus entered Jerusalem riding on a donkey days before his crucifixion (Matthew 21:1-17; Mark 11:1-11; Luke 19:29-40; John 12:1, 12-19).

The sacrifice was to be killed publicly (Exodus 12:6).
Jesus was killed publicly.

The sacrifice was to be killed on Passover (Exodus 12:6).
Jesus was crucified on Passover (Luke 22:7-8).

The sacrifice was to be roasted by fire (Exodus 12:8).
Jesus took the full judgment of God upon himself (Isaiah 53:10; 2 Corinthians 5:21).

The sacrifice was to be dead by twilight (Exodus 12:6).
Jesus died before evening (John 19:31).

The sacrifice was not to have any broken bones (Exodus 12:46).
Jesus did not have any broken bones (Psalm 34:20; John 19:31-34).

The sacrifice was to be consumed by the end of the day (Exodus 12:10).
Jesus's body was buried quickly in Joseph's tomb before the Sabbath began at nightfall (John 19:40-42).

The Israelites were saved by the blood on the top and sides of their doorposts (Exodus 12:7, 12).
We are saved by the sacrificial blood of Christ (Ephesians 1:7).

The sacrifice was not to be eaten by foreigners (Exodus 12:43).
Jesus came first to save the household of Israel (Matthew 15:24).

During the exodus, Gentiles also left with the Hebrew people (Exodus 12:38).
Gentiles can be grafted in and saved (Romans 11:17-18).

The calendar was changed because of Passover (Exodus 12:2).
The world calendar is divided between BC and AD.

The Passover designated the new year (Exodus 12:2).
The shed blood of Jesus ushered in the new covenant/New Testament (Luke 22:20).

Tabernacle Typology

A careful study of the layout of the tabernacle as well as other details connected to it (colors, materials, implements, etc.) from Exodus chapters 25–40 point to the cross and other redemptive themes of the future Messiah and God's plan of salvation for humanity. Hebrews chapter 8 explains the typological link between the tabernacle (and the sacrificial system) and the prophetic fulfillment found in Christ.

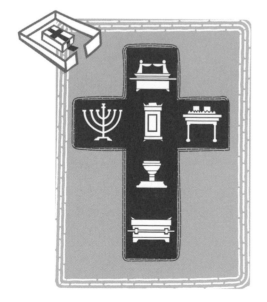

In addition, the very layout of the tabernacle resembles a cross. Long before death by crucifixion was invented, there was a curious and compelling symbolism associated with the cross-like layout of the tabernacle. Today, as we view the Old Testament through the lens of the cross, we see that it was prophetically hidden there in plain sight.

Viewing the tabernacle as a cross, we can now see that the priest would enter the courtyard of the tabernacle at the foot of the cross through the sacrifice of an innocent representative. Just beyond the altar was a basin for washing. Through the sacrifice, the priest was made clean and could enter the presence of God. Once inside the holy place, to one side was a table with bread. To the other side was a lamp burning. Jesus is the bread of life and light of the world. Beyond this area was the holy of holies (complete with the ark of the covenant)—clearly a representation of the temple in heaven (Revelation 11:19).

The Second Coming Foreshadowed

While there is no specific verse connecting the two events, one can't miss the typological parallels between Exodus chapter 32 and later details we learn about the return of Christ. The historical Moses is a type of Christ. While Moses was up on Mount Sinai getting the Ten Commandments, he was gone longer than the Israelites expected. When the people became anxious and worried that Moses's mountaintop meeting with God was taking too long, they doubted and mocked God's promises, and turned to man-centered ungodliness and idolatry. When Moses returned, he found them involved in immoral, occultic behavior. He gathered those who were "for the LORD" (Exodus 32:26), then ordered swift judgment on the rest of the people, who were not for the Lord (verses 27-29).

During the future tribulation period, many people will practice immorality and occultic behavior. After the first set of judgments from God have already commenced, we read this in Revelation 9:20-21: "The rest of mankind who were not killed by these plagues still did not repent of the work of their hands; they did not stop worshiping demons, and idols of gold, silver, bronze, stone and wood—idols that cannot see or hear or walk. Nor did they repent of their murders, their magic arts, their sexual immorality or their thefts."

Even prior to the tribulation period, we find some prophetic parallels. In 2 Peter 3:3-4, we read, "Above all, you must understand that in the last days scoffers will come, scoffing and following their own evil desires. They will say, 'Where is this "coming" he promised? Ever since our ancestors died, everything goes on as it has since the beginning of creation.'"

Jesus's parable of the 10 minas (Luke 19:11-27) depicts a "man of noble birth" as being gone to a distant country for an extended period. Before he left, he put his servants in charge of some of his wealth, instructing them to invest wisely while he was gone. During his time away, some would heed his advice, while others would ignore it. Upon his return, those who invested wisely would be rewarded, while those who did not would be punished.

In other words, this foretold that Jesus would be gone for an extended period and many would do nothing, stop awaiting his return, and turn away from the things of God. We read in other passages about a great apostasy— a major drifting away from truth and an increasing worldliness within the church as we near the time of the Lord's return (Luke 18:8; 2 Thessalonians 2:3; 2 Timothy 3:1-5; 4:3; Revelation 3:16-20).

Many passages in the Old Testament present prophetic types or foreshadows of the Messiah in relation to both his first and second comings. The fulfillments of these prophetic types serve as strong evidence of the divine origin of the Bible.

LEVITICUS

LEVITICUS (859 TOTAL VERSES)

PROPHECIES/VERSES	FULFILLED/VERSES	TYPES	TOTAL PROPHETIC CONTENT	PERCENTAGE
10/158	0/0	5/64	161 VERSES	19%

NOTE: MUCH OF CHAPTERS 1-9 (SACRIFICIAL SYSTEM) COULD BE CONSIDERED TYPOLOGY.

In many ways, Leviticus is an extension of the section in Exodus that deals with the tabernacle. After several chapters in Exodus about the construction and layout of the tabernacle, Leviticus provides specific details related to priestly duties, religious life, and other general regulations for the Jewish people. It is the "how-to" manual for living under the Old Testament law. The book derives its name from the tribe of Levi—the priestly tribe. The tribe itself is not emphasized in the book, but the regulations given in Leviticus were designed to guide the Israelites on how to worship God and live in a way that honored him.

In terms of prophetic significance, there are a few important things to point out—the most obvious being that the regular sacrifices all pointed to the ultimate sacrifice of Jesus Christ on the cross. Other important prophetic themes include the Lord's feasts in chapter 23 and the densely packed prophetic narrative of chapter 26

The Lord's Feasts

In Leviticus 23, the Lord designated seven feast days the people were to observe. The feast days, or literally, God's appointed festivals, celebrated God's work in the past and pointed to future events connected with the first and second comings of the Messiah. The feasts are separated into two seasons: the spring rains begin the harvest season, and the fall rains end it. Hosea 6 hints at the first and second comings of Christ. In verse 3 we read, "He will come to us like the rain, like the latter and former rain to the earth" (NKJV).

In prophetic terms, the early feasts of spring correspond to key events of Jesus's first coming, while the fall feasts correspond to key events related to his second coming. The inauguration and consummation of God's work of salvation are clearly depicted in the two sets of feasts and separated by the summer months, which represent the period of time between the two advents. In Colossians 2:17, Paul informs us that the festivals were given as "a shadow of the things that were to come." Then he drives the point home by saying, "The reality, however, is found in Christ."

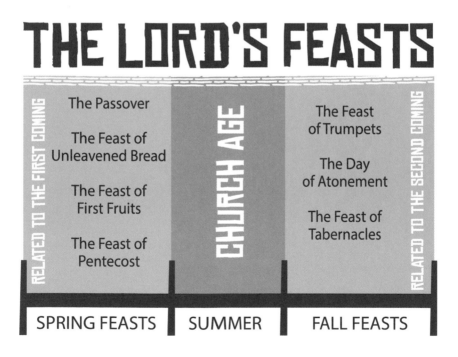

THE LORD'S FEASTS

RELATED TO THE FIRST COMING

The Passover

The Feast of Unleavened Bread

The Feast of First Fruits

The Feast of Pentecost

CHURCH AGE

The Feast of Trumpets

The Day of Atonement

The Feast of Tabernacles

RELATED TO THE SECOND COMING

SPRING FEASTS   SUMMER   FALL FEASTS

Power-Packed Prophecies of Blessing and Cursing

The second-to-last chapter of Leviticus provides a series of detailed prophetic promises and warnings to Israel. In Leviticus 26 are many details about how God would bless the people of Israel for their obedience, along with many other details about what would happen if they disobeyed God's laws and decrees. The punishments for disobedience include sickness, loss of goods to enemies, attacks and oppression by enemies, crop failures, the ruining of the land and cities, starvation, and dispersion and mistreatment in other nations.

Indeed, these prophetic blessings were experienced by the Jewish nation as they first took the Promised Land and increased in number—as well as the consequences when they disobeyed the Lord repeatedly and faced defeat, captivity, dispersion, and mistreatment everywhere they went. Fortunately, the end of the chapter includes a prophetic promise that the Lord would remember the Jewish people and the land, and that there would remain a remnant of his people:

> When they are in the land of their enemies, I will not reject them or abhor them so as to destroy them completely, breaking my covenant with them. I am the LORD their God. But for their sake I will remember the covenant with their ancestors whom I brought out of Egypt in the sight of the nations to be their God. I am the LORD (verses 44-45).

NUMBERS

NUMBERS (1,288 TOTAL VERSES)

PROPHECIES/VERSES	FULFILLED/VERSES	TYPES	TOTAL PROPHETIC CONTENT	PERCENTAGE
38/69	8/62	6/116	247 VERSES	19%

END-TIMES PROPHECIES: 1 (1 VERSE) | NOTE: MUCH OF CHAPTERS 3-9 COULD ALSO BE TYPOLOGY.

Bird's-Eye View of the Cross

The arrangement of the 12 tribes, as detailed in Numbers 2, form the shape of the cross. If the subtle cross shape I described in the section on Exodus (see page 44) was not compelling enough, consider the cross shape found

in the book of Numbers. When you carefully lay out the tribes (and the population count for each as described in Numbers 2), the picture of a giant cross emerges. The top of the cross points eastward toward the Promised Land. At the center of this giant cross is the cross formation within the tabernacle. This should get our attention because the method of putting people to death on a cross was not invented for a very long time after Numbers was written. In Scripture, we're not introduced to the cross until we reach the Gospels!

Surprising "Idolatry"?

The seemingly idolatrous use of the raised snake in Numbers 21 also foreshadowed the cross. When a plague of poisonous snakes was killing the people, God told Moses to "make a snake and put it up on a pole; anyone who is bitten can look at it and live" (verse 8). This odd event in the biblical narrative is left hanging there like an unfinished riddle or an unexplained object lesson—that is, until we get to the New Testament.

Roughly 1,500 years later, the riddle was explained and the object lesson made sense. In John 3:14-15, Jesus said, "Just as Moses lifted up the snake in the wilderness, so the Son of Man must be lifted up, that everyone who believes may have eternal life in him."

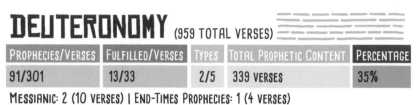

DEUTERONOMY (959 TOTAL VERSES)

PROPHECIES/VERSES	FULFILLED/VERSES	TYPES	TOTAL PROPHETIC CONTENT	PERCENTAGE
91/301	13/33	2/5	339 VERSES	35%

MESSIANIC: 2 (10 VERSES) | END-TIMES PROPHECIES: 1 (4 VERSES)

This book title (taken from the Greek Septuagint, or Greek translation of the Old Testament) means "second law-giving," but the original Hebrew title translates to "words" and was a term used in reference to treaties of the day. Indeed, the format of the book follows the pattern of a treaty, focusing on the responsibilities of God's chosen people. Many of the laws previously set forth are repeated in the book of Deuteronomy.

When someone teaches from the Old Testament, Deuteronomy is not one of the more common texts chosen. But there are some hidden prophetic gems within this often-overlooked book of the Torah! Here are a few examples.

In Deuteronomy 4:30-31, there is a specific end-time prophecy about Israel: "When you are in distress and all these things have happened to you, then in later days you will return to the LORD your God and obey him. For the LORD your God is a merciful God; he will not abandon or destroy you or forget the covenant with your ancestors, which he confirmed to them by oath."

These two verses highlight a theme that readers will see emphasized in this book: God's unconditional future promises to Israel still stand and these prophecies will come to pass just as foretold. This may seem like an obvious conclusion if we take the plain sense of the language God used in various prophecies related to Israel and the Jewish people, but the idea that God has specific modern-day and future plans for Israel is a minority view among many Protestants and in Catholic circles as well. The official theological stance of many churches and denominations today is that the church has replaced Israel and that all the Old Testament promises to Israel are now symbolically pointing to the church.

I'll share more on this as this book progresses, but the forever nature of God's promise to Israel has its roots in the Abrahamic covenant and other foundational areas of the Torah, including here in the book of Deuteronomy.

God's Name on Jerusalem

In Deuteronomy 12:10-11, we find a curious prophecy in the context of the future taking of the Promised Land (at the time of the prophecy):

> You will cross the Jordan and settle in the land the LORD your God is giving you as an inheritance, and he will give you rest from all your enemies around you so that you will live in safety. Then to the place the LORD your God will choose as a dwelling for his Name—there you are to bring everything I command you: your burnt offerings and sacrifices, your tithes and special gifts, and all the choice possessions you have vowed to the LORD.

Did you catch that? God said Jerusalem would become a dwelling for his name (see also Deuteronomy 12:5, 21; 14:23-24; 16:2, 6, 11; 26:2; 1 Kings 11:36; 14:21; 2 Kings 21:4, 7). That's a pretty big deal, but it's easily over-looked. In 2 Kings 21:7, God adds the detail that he would put his name there "forever." A name represents someone's character and promises. Our word is our bond. God's name is bound to Jerusalem!

Some have even asserted that the three valleys in Jerusalem (Hinnom, Tyropeoeon, and Kidron) form the Hebrew letter *shin*, which is the twenty-first letter of the Hebrew alphabet. It looks similar to an English *W* and can represent Shaddai, a name of God that means "God Almighty."

Blessings and Curses

If you will recall from what we learned earlier, Leviticus 26 is a densely detailed chapter of blessings and curses. All of these blessings and curses have indeed come to pass in the history of the Jewish people from that time to today. Here in Deuteronomy, we find a similar passage that spans chapters 28–30. Chapter 28 has the most prophetic content and is very similar to

Leviticus 26—it speaks of fruitfulness and success in times of obedience; and in times of disobedience, it speaks of sickness, barrenness, drought, attacks from enemies, being scattered to the nations, and mistreatment while in those lands. Both Leviticus 26 and Deuteronomy 28 end with the promise that God would remember his covenant with Israel and would not break it.

Within the context of God's prophetic narrative as it relates to Israel, he emphasizes personal responsibility and the fact that each individual must choose to follow God's ways. In Deuteronomy 29:19-21, we read,

> When such a person hears the words of this oath and they invoke a blessing on themselves, thinking, "I will be safe, even though I persist in going my own way," they will bring disaster on the watered land as well as the dry. The LORD will never be willing to forgive them; his wrath and zeal will burn against them. All the curses written in this book will fall on them, and the LORD will blot out their names from under heaven. The LORD will single them out from all the tribes of Israel for disaster, according to all the curses of the covenant written in this Book of the Law.

Paul emphasizes this in Romans chapters 9–11. The clear theme throughout Scripture is that God has a prophetic end-times purpose for a literal national Israel and literal Jewish people. Regardless of what happens to the Jewish people, there will always be a remnant who survive and who believe in Jesus Christ. By the end of the tribulation period, all surviving Jewish people will accept Christ as their Savior. These Jewish survivors of the tribulation period (along with Gentile believers and Old Testament believers) will usher in the kingdom age, where they will rule with Christ for 1,000 years (Revelation 20:1-7). We'll study more about the millennial kingdom in the upcoming section on the prophets and in the chapter on the book of Revelation.

Parting Prophetic Words of the Torah

Near the end of the final book of the Torah, in Deuteronomy 33—Moses concludes his writings with a prophetic blessing to each of the tribes. This is fitting because Genesis (the first book of the Torah) ends with a similar blessing from Jacob/Israel to each of the tribes represented by his sons. So both the first and last of the foundational books of the Bible contain prophetic chapters about the future of the tribes of Israel toward the end of each book.

A MOSAIC MADE BY GOD

Is it any wonder that the New Jerusalem—our future living quarters as believers—has 12 gates with the names of the tribes of Israel (Revelation 21:12)? Is it any wonder that the 12 foundations named after the 12 Jewish apostles are made of precious stones (Revelation 21:19-20), just like the 12 precious stones in the priestly ephod described in Exodus 28:17-21?

The first five books of the Bible are truly the prophetic, thematic, and theological foundation of everything else we discover in the pages of Scripture. A careful study of Bible prophecy highlights this eye-opening truth in amazing detail. It forces us to slow down long enough to appreciate the beauty, design, and trustworthiness of the world's greatest book!

If you are familiar with art terms, you may recall that *mosaic* is an art form in which the medium used is small broken pieces of colored glass, stones, or other hard objects. When viewing a mosaic up close, you notice the rough spots, the disjointed appearance of seemingly random objects placed near one another. But when you take a few steps back to view the entire finished design, a beautiful picture emerges.

The term *mosaic* relates to the life of Moses. As with us, each small vignette of his life seemed like a stand-alone event or trial. With all the ups and downs, twists and turns, setbacks and victories that took place in his life, the many individual incidents Moses experienced may appear, at first glance, like a bunch of rough, broken pieces. But as we view the panoramic sweep of Moses's life—and the five books of the Torah which he wrote—the many pieces fit together like a beautiful, foundational, and prophetic masterpiece around which the rest of the divine art gallery was built!

Fulfilled Prophecy
Via Messy History

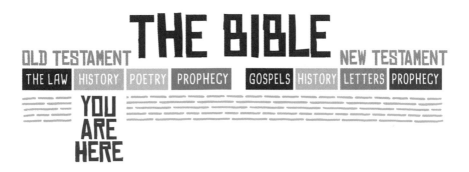

*Be strong and courageous, because you will lead these people
to inherit the land I swore to their ancestors to give them.*

—JOSHUA 1:6

History is messy. The history of our lives is often messy too. But nothing can stop the foreordained decrees of God. Regardless of the influences of the world, the flesh, and the devil, all prophetic rivers flow to the sea of God's omniscient purpose.

This chapter includes Joshua, Judges, Ruth, 1 and 2 Samuel, 1 and 2 Kings, 1 and 2 Chronicles, Ezra, Nehemiah, and Esther. These books encompass roughly 900 years of Jewish history (1400–473 BC) and cover many key events, including Israel's entry into and conquest of Canaan, the rise of the judges, the reign of King David (and other kings), the dividing of the kingdom, the fall of Jerusalem, the Babylonian captivity, the release from Babylon 70 years later, the deliverance of the Jews in Persia, and the rebuilding of

Jerusalem and the temple. In fulfillment of prophecy, all these events progressively laid the foundation for the first coming of Jesus.

As the billions of historical details took place, they were all heading toward a foreordained outcome: the promised arrival of the Messiah. Prophecy does not happen in a vacuum. In many ways, the History section of the Old Testament chronicles the progression of historical details that prepared the way for the coming of the long-awaited offspring of the woman, who was first promised in Genesis 3:15. There are several important prophetic themes in this section of the Old Testament, and I have highlighted a few of them for you in the following pages. Let's begin by considering the prophetic content in the book of Joshua.

JOSHUA

JOSHUA (658 TOTAL VERSES)

PROPHECIES/VERSES	FULFILLED/VERSES	TYPES	TOTAL PROPHETIC CONTENT	PERCENTAGE
25/41	29/85	1/1	127 VERSES	19%

From the first revelation of the Abrahamic promise in Genesis chapter 12, God foretold that Abraham's descendants would obtain the Promised Land. In verses 6-7, we read, "Abram traveled through the land as far as the site of the great tree of Moreh at Shechem. At that time the Canaanites were in the land. The LORD appeared to Abram and said, 'To your offspring I will give this land.' So he built an altar there to the LORD, who had appeared to him."

Entrance to the Promised Land

The book of Joshua is a continuation of the narrative of the exodus and the 40 years of wandering in the desert until the time was right to enter the Promised Land. At its heart, the book of Joshua is the historical record of fulfilled prophecy. Joshua and his generation were witnesses to—and participants in—fulfilled prophecy! The book of Joshua chronicles this process in three main parts: entering the land (chapters 1–12), dividing the land (13–22), and Joshua's parting message and death (23–24). Joshua was also a clear type of Christ. His name is the Greek equivalent of the name *Jesus*. Furthermore, Joshua would lead his people into the Promised Land, just as Christ would lead his people into their ultimate rest (see Hebrews 4:8).

Joshua 21:43-45 sums up the prophetic nature of the book very well. There, we read,

> The LORD gave Israel all the land he had sworn to give their ances-
> tors, and they took possession of it and settled there. The LORD
> gave them rest on every side, just as he had sworn to their ancestors.
> Not one of their enemies withstood them; the LORD gave all their
> enemies into their hands. Not one of all the LORD's good prom-
> ises to Israel failed; every one was fulfilled.

In addition to the broad prophetic narrative of Joshua, we also find some very clear symbolism conveyed by the red cord hung from Rahab's window. This woman trusted Joshua's promise of protection and deliverance, and she took faith-based action. Her name later appears in the genealogy of Jesus (Matthew 1:5).

The Practical Benefit of Prophecy Modeled by Joshua

I would also like to point out how practical a study of Bible prophecy is to our daily faith walk with the Lord. We see in the recorded narrative of the 12 spies who did a military reconnaissance of the land of Canaan that Caleb and Joshua were the only two willing to take action based on Bible proph-ecy. When we read the account in Numbers 13:26-33, we find that ten of the scouts were afraid of the Canaanites and viewed the situation from a human perspective. But Joshua and Caleb viewed the situation through the eyes of faith—based on Bible prophecy!

Through Moses, God had told the Israelites multiple times that the Prom-ised Land would be delivered to them. Joshua and Caleb believed these proph-ecies and put their faith into action. In verse 30, we read, "Caleb silenced the people before Moses and said, 'We should go up and take possession of the land, for we can certainly do it.'"

We can learn a practical lesson from this: God's prophecies are God's promises. God is a promise-keeper, and we can take him at his plain word.

Prophecies are fulfilled literally, not figuratively. God is not the author of confusion, but of clarity. A proper understanding of Bible prophecy always leads to clarity and hope—not confusion and fear.

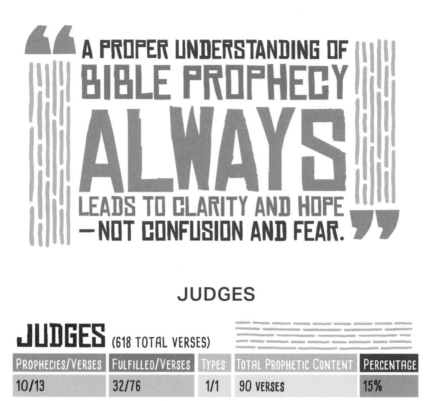

"A PROPER UNDERSTANDING OF BIBLE PROPHECY ALWAYS LEADS TO CLARITY AND HOPE —NOT CONFUSION AND FEAR."

JUDGES

JUDGES (618 TOTAL VERSES)				
PROPHECIES/VERSES	FULFILLED/VERSES	TYPES	TOTAL PROPHETIC CONTENT	PERCENTAGE
10/13	32/76	1/1	90 VERSES	15%

In Judges, we see God working out his prophetic stage-setting during a time of lawlessness when "everyone did as they saw fit" (Judges 21:25). This mirrors our day (2 Timothy 3:1-4) and the cultural conditions during the future tribulation period, when lawlessness will reach its peak after the restraining influence of the church is removed via the rapture (2 Thessalonians 2:6-7).

In the middle of the judgments described in the book of Revelation, we read this in 9:21: "Nor did they repent of their murders, their magic arts, their sexual immorality or their thefts." In times of lawlessness—when God's Word and his ways are not heeded—chaos ensues, yet often people continue to do what is right in their own eyes. We find this delusion at play in Paul's description of God's judgment in the New Testament. I'll discuss this more in chapter 12.

RUTH

RUTH (85 TOTAL VERSES)		
TYPES	TOTAL PROPHETIC CONTENT	PERCENTAGE
3/19	19 VERSES	22%

There are only two books in the Bible that are named after women—Ruth and Esther. Both books are in the historical section of the Old Testament and contain profound typology related to Jesus. In the book of Ruth, a Gentile from Moab entered the genealogy of Jesus through her marriage to Boaz—the great-grandfather of King David. We also discover that Rahab—the prostitute turned faithful follower (see Joshua overview earlier)—was Boaz's mother (Matthew 1:5)!

In Ruth, a Jewish kinsman-redeemer named Boaz is a type of Christ—the Jewish kinsman-redeemer who secured our salvation. Ruth was a Gentile bride—a clear foreshadow of the church in the New Testament. In Ephesians 5:23, we read, "The husband is the head of the wife as Christ is the head of the church, his body, of which he is the Savior." Then later in verses 31-32 of the same chapter, we read, "For this reason a man will leave his father and mother and be united to his wife, and the two will become one flesh. This is a profound mystery—but I am talking about Christ and the church."

KINSMAN REDEEMER = TYPE OF CHRIST

In ancient Israel, if a person or land were sold into bondage, specific requirements were laid out for how they were to be bought back (that is, redeemed). A close relative (known as a kinsman-redeemer) who met these requirements had the option of redeeming the person or property, if they wished (see also Leviticus 25; Deuteronomy 25).

- First, the kinsman-redeemer had to be a close blood relative (Deuteronomy 25:5).

- Second, he had to be able to pay the full price of redemption.
- Third, he had to be willing to pay the price.
- Fourth, the redeemer had to be free himself, not owing any debt elsewhere.

So, the kinsman-redeemer buys back people and property via his own sacrificial payment. John picks up this symbolism in the book of Revelation, where we find Jesus—our Kinsman-Redeemer—reclaiming his property as he opens the seals to the title deed to earth at the beginning of the future seven-year tribulation period (see Revelation chapters 5–6).

1 AND 2 SAMUEL

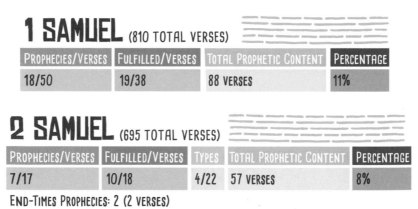

1 SAMUEL (810 TOTAL VERSES)

PROPHECIES/VERSES	FULFILLED/VERSES	TOTAL PROPHETIC CONTENT	PERCENTAGE
18/50	19/38	88 VERSES	11%

2 SAMUEL (695 TOTAL VERSES)

PROPHECIES/VERSES	FULFILLED/VERSES	TYPES	TOTAL PROPHETIC CONTENT	PERCENTAGE
7/17	10/18	4/22	57 VERSES	8%

END-TIMES PROPHECIES: 2 (2 VERSES)

In 1 and 2 Samuel, we meet an amazing figure whom the book is named after. We also learn about the life of King David. Both Samuel and David were types or foreshadows of the Messiah. Samuel was a type of Christ in that he was a prophet, a priest, and a ruler (serving as judge/protector between the time of the judges and the installment of Saul as Israel's first king). Samuel was the only figure in the Old Testament who held all three mantles. Various prophecies in the Bible tell us that the Messiah would be a prophet

(Deuteronomy 18:15; Matthew 21:11; Luke 7:16; 24:27; John 4:19;, 6:14; 7:40; Hebrews 7:17), priest (Jeremiah 31:31-34; Hebrews 7:17; 9:11-14), and king (Genesis 49:10; Matthew 22:42–45; Hebrews 7:17).

David was also a key type of Christ, and his kingdom was a foreshadow of the yet-future millennial kingdom detailed in the books of the prophets and the book of Revelation. Many prophecies in the Old Testament connected David to the Messiah. I'll detail many of those prophecies in upcoming chapters—particularly as we study the Psalms and Isaiah.

The Davidic Covenant

Prophecy is progressively revealed. In other words, it is given in increments, with each new revelation building upon previous prophecies. For example, after the fall, mankind knew the Messiah would come through the offspring of a woman (Genesis 3:15). About 2,000 years later, God revealed the Messiah would come through the line of Abraham. Then about another 1,000 years later, we discover (first here in 2 Samuel 7, then later in 1 Chronicles 17:11-14 and 2 Chronicles 6:16) that the Messiah would come through the line of David and that David's kingdom would last forever.

The Davidic covenant contains three major promises: First, that David's lineage would endure forever (2 Samuel 7:16; 2 Chronicles 21:7; Psalm 89:3–4, 36). Second, that David's kingdom (though paused/interrupted in history) would continue permanently (2 Samuel 7:16). Third, God promised that David's throne would never permanently pass away (verse 16). In its Old Testament form, David's kingdom eventually experienced civil war, captivity, and an 1,878-year worldwide dispersion, yet—just as foretold in many Old Testament prophecies—it has become a nation again in modern times and will experience every kingdom promise of the Davidic covenant in the future millennial kingdom. As we walk through Old Testament history, we simply cannot get away from of the way Bible prophecy compellingly connects the Old Testament to the New Testament.

The Mountain Peaks of Bible Prophecy

Another key principle of Bible prophecy is that many prophetic passages hit only the high points of what will happen. Experts refer to this as

MOUNTAIN PEAKS

SIDE VIEW

VALLEY OF TIME

the mountain peaks of prophecy. One prophecy may have many key details that will occur hundreds or even thousands of years apart. We don't see the details of the valley between the peaks, but the peaks are there nonetheless. They serve as key prophetic markers that stand out among the thousands of other details. Just as a mountain peak guides the hiker's journey, the mountain peaks of prophecy guide us as we watch prophetic events unfold today.

One final key point related to the Davidic covenant: As with the Abrahamic covenant, this additional covenant is unconditional. It is wholly dependent on the faithfulness of God for its fulfillment. Through all the twists and turns of history, the impact of disobedient people, and spiritual warfare coming against the covenant, nothing can stop God's prophecies from being fulfilled. He is a faithful promise-keeper. This should give us great joy in the church age as we trust the promises and prophecies God has given to us!

1 AND 2 KINGS

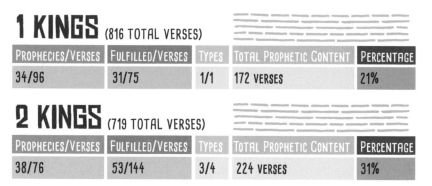

1 KINGS (816 TOTAL VERSES)

PROPHECIES/VERSES	FULFILLED/VERSES	TYPES	TOTAL PROPHETIC CONTENT	PERCENTAGE
34/96	31/75	1/1	172 VERSES	21%

2 KINGS (719 TOTAL VERSES)

PROPHECIES/VERSES	FULFILLED/VERSES	TYPES	TOTAL PROPHETIC CONTENT	PERCENTAGE
38/76	53/144	3/4	224 VERSES	31%

Finally, in 1 and 2 Kings and 1 and 2 Chronicles, we meet two of the Old Testament's most famous prophets—Elijah and Elisha, who clearly foreshadow John the Baptist and Jesus. Elijah is likely one of the two witnesses who will show up in Jerusalem during the future tribulation period

(Revelation 11). There are also several other key prophetic sections in these Old Testament books, which I describe below.

In 1 Kings chapter 9, the Lord appeared to Solomon to reaffirm his unconditional promise to his father, David. But here, we gain some added detail. Even though the Davidic promise is permanent, disobedience could derail the kingdom in the interim. Solomon was given the choice to continue in his father's obedient path or turn away from God by worshipping and serving other gods and being cut off from the land (9:4-7). Sadly, as we'll learn, Solomon chose the latter (1 Kings 10–11), and the kingdom suffered the temporary yet horrific consequences.

In 1 Kings 11, we read this clear prophetic promise from the Lord: "I will humble David's descendants because of this, but not forever" (verse 39). The mountain peaks of prophecy would prevail. These are key prophetic details that—along with many others we'll discover in the major and minor prophets—drive home the point that God's promises to the people of Israel through the Abrahamic and Davidic covenants are permanent. In the New Testament, Paul the apostle affirmed this in Romans 11:29, where he wrote—in the specific context of Israel's church-age role and future—that "God's gifts and his call are irrevocable."

Enigmatic Elijah

In 1 Kings chapters 17–19, we're introduced to the prophet Elijah. This mysterious figure appears out of nowhere in the narrative of the book and performs some incredible miracles during a dark time when the false prophets of Baal worship influenced the kingdom. Spiritual warfare and miraculous events seem to arise at various plot points along the path of God's overarching narrative. Creation and the fall. The flood of Noah's day. Moses and the exodus. The period featuring Elijah and Elisha. The birth of Christ. The death and resurrection of Christ. The birth of the church. Then finally, during the future tribulation period and other events related to the end times.

There's another prophetic principle to observe here. Between the giving of a prophecy and its fulfillment, there are often long, seemingly dull periods of spiritual activity as history plays out and the stage is set for the fulfillment of prophecy. During the stage-setting historical periods, people tend to lose sight of God's promises and begin to scoff and turn to worldly ways. Then at just the right time, God intervenes, and prophecy is fulfilled in spectacular ways.

MOUNTAIN PEAKS

Our job is to trust God's mountain-peak prophetic promises as we live in the valley watching the stage being set.

Peter pointed out that this is exactly what will happen in relation to the fulfillment of last-days prophecies. He wrote,

> Above all, you must understand that in the last days scoffers will come, scoffing and following their own evil desires. They will say, "Where is this 'coming' he promised? Ever since our ancestors died, everything goes on as it has since the beginning of creation." But they deliberately forget that long ago by God's word the heavens came into being and the earth was formed out of water and by water. By these waters also the world of that time was deluged and destroyed. By the same word the present heavens and earth are reserved for fire, being kept for the day of judgment and destruction of the ungodly (2 Peter 3:3-7).

A Preview of the Rapture

One interesting prophetic event that foreshadows the future rapture of the church is Elijah's rapture in 2 Kings 2:11-12. We use the term *rapture* to describe the future event spoken of in 1 Thessalonians 4:13-18 and 1 Corinthians 15:50-52, where we read that the dead will be raised and given glorified bodies, then living believers will be "caught up" to be with them. The Greek word for "caught up" is *harpazo*, which means "a sudden physical snatching away." When the Bible was translated into Latin, the Greek word *harpazo* was translated *rapturo*, from which we get our modern English word *rapture*.

We see an early individual glimpse of this future corporate event in 2 Kings 2. Here, we find a few details that foreshadow our future rapture as believers in the church age. First, people knew and believed Elijah would be taken up (verses 3, 5, 9). Second, it happened very suddenly (verse 11). Third, it involved the armies of heaven (verse 12). In other words, it was a spiritual warfare event—much like the future sudden evacuation of church-age believers from the territory of the prince of the power of the air (see Ephesians 2:1-2).

1 AND 2 CHRONICLES

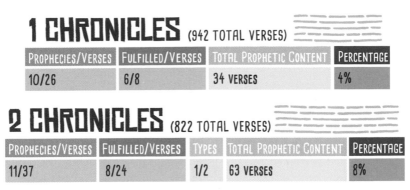

1 CHRONICLES (942 TOTAL VERSES)

Prophecies/Verses	Fulfilled/Verses	Total Prophetic Content	Percentage
10/26	6/8	34 VERSES	4%

2 CHRONICLES (822 TOTAL VERSES)

Prophecies/Verses	Fulfilled/Verses	Types	Total Prophetic Content	Percentage
11/37	8/24	1/2	63 VERSES	8%

Even though the books of 1 and 2 Chronicles cover the same historical time frame as 1 and 2 Samuel and 1 and 2 Kings, it does so in a different way by focusing mainly on the positive aspects of the kingly lineage of David (and, for the most part, leaving out details about the evil kings during that period). In terms of prophetic content, there are a few key passages worth noting.

In 1 Chronicles 17, Nathan the prophet received a compelling prophetic revelation from the Lord after he and David discussed David's passion to build a temple for the Lord. In verses 9-14, we read,

> I will provide a place for my people Israel and will plant them so that they can have a home of their own and no longer be disturbed. Wicked people will not oppress them anymore, as they did at the beginning and have done ever since the time I appointed leaders over my people Israel. I will also subdue all your enemies. I declare to you that the LORD will build a house for you: When your days are over and you go to be with your ancestors, I will raise up your offspring to succeed you, one of your own sons, and I will establish his kingdom. He is the one who will build a house for me, and I will establish his throne forever. I will be his father, and he will be my son. I will never take my love away from him, as I took it away from your predecessor. I will set him over my house and my kingdom forever; his throne will be established forever.

Notice the word "forever" is used three times. Also notice that this is not talking about David's son Solomon, but a future descendant who would arise sometime after David's death. This passage can be taken at face value. It is not figurative language, and there is no inkling of a possibility that this unconditional prophecy was to be taken any other way but literally.

Small Beginnings

Another fascinating account is recorded in 1 Chronicles 21:18-30, where we read that David purchases a small plot of land that would later become the site of the temple. Prophetically speaking, the temple has always played a significant role in God's plans for his people. This small beginning would prove to be an important prophetic theme in Scripture.

In 2 Chronicles, the temple is prominently featured. The first temple, built by Solomon, was destroyed by the Babylonians in 586 BC. After the Babylonian exile, Zerubbabel led the people in their efforts to rebuild the temple (ca. 515 BC). Around 20 BC, King Herod began enhancing and enlarging the temple and temple complex. This massive wonder existed during the time of Jesus and was destroyed in AD 70 by the Romans (as predicted by Jesus in Matthew 24:1-2).

The temple remains a key feature in end-times prophecy as well. At the midpoint of the future seven-year tribulation, the antichrist will enter the temple and defile it. This is what is known as the abomination of desolation. More on this when we get to Daniel 9, Matthew 24, and the book of Revelation. We will also study the detailed information in the last several chapters of Ezekiel, where we discover mention of a fourth and final temple—the future temple of the millennial kingdom. And all of this began with David's modest purchase of a small threshing floor as recorded in 1 Chronicles 21.

People, Land, and Promises

In 2 Chronicles 7, we bump into one incredibly prophetic section of Scripture that includes details related to the Abrahamic covenant, the Davidic covenant, and the prophetic warnings of blessings and curses in Leviticus 26 and Deuteronomy 28 affirming the permanent nature of the prophetic promises.

In 2 Chronicles 7:19-22, we read,

If you turn away and forsake the decrees and commands I have given you and go off to serve other gods and worship them, then I will uproot Israel from my land, which I have given them, and will reject this temple I have consecrated for my Name. I will make it a byword and an object of ridicule among all peoples. This temple will become a heap of rubble. All who pass by will be appalled and say, "Why has the LORD done such a thing to this land and to this temple?" People will answer, "Because they have forsaken the LORD, the God of their ancestors, who brought them out of Egypt, and have embraced other gods, worshiping and serving them—that is why he brought all this disaster on them."

God warns and he is patient, but at some point, he must act. Though God sent prophets to warn the people, when they refused to repent, his only choice was to bring judgment. That is exactly what happened in the history of Israel (as with the flood of Noah's day and the destruction of Sodom and Gomorrah). We see this pattern in crisp detail in 2 Chronicles 36:15-16, where we read,

The LORD, the God of their ancestors, sent word to them through his messengers again and again, because he had pity on his people and on his dwelling place. But they mocked God's messengers, despised his words and scoffed at his prophets until the wrath of the LORD was aroused against his people and there was no remedy.

From Genesis to Revelation, the pattern of God's judgment is the same. He is patient. He warns. His grace is extended as far as possible. But if there is no repentance, no change of heart, then judgment must come.

EZRA

EZRA (280 TOTAL VERSES)

Fulfilled/Verses	Types	Total Prophetic Content	Percentage
10/129	1/4	133 verses	48%

Thankfully, God kept his unconditional promises to Israel and the Jewish people. Though he had to judge them, he promised to restore them and put a descendant on the throne of a future kingdom. The historical books of Ezra, Nehemiah, and Esther tell the story of what happened when the Jewish people returned from their captivity in Babylon.

In Ezra, we read about how God kept the Davidic line of the Messiah and preserved the religious aspects of life as he restored his people to their temple and land in fulfillment of prophecy. After 70 years of captivity in Babylon (as prophesied in Jeremiah 29:10), King Cyrus of Persia made a proclamation that the Jewish exiles could return home to rebuild their city and temple (Ezra 1:1-4). The return took place in three phases—two of them detailed in Ezra (led first by Zerubbabel ca. 536 BC, then roughly 80 years later by Ezra the priest, ca. 457 BC), and the phase roughly 13 years later (ca. 444 BC) as documented in the book of Nehemiah (see below). The first two returns focused on the restoration of the temple and the people's religious life, while the third concentrated on rebuilding the walls of Jerusalem.

Here we have the fulfillment of prophecy playing out in the history of the Jewish people—the captivity, then the return. Unfortunately, this would happen again on a much larger scale with a much longer dispersion—1,878 years to be exact. From AD 70 to 1948, the Jewish people had no home. We'll discuss some amazing prophecies related to the rebirth of Israel in upcoming chapters, but here in Ezra we find the restoration of the people from their first dispersion, just as God promised.

NEHEMIAH

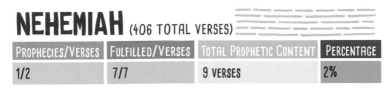

NEHEMIAH (406 TOTAL VERSES)

PROPHECIES/VERSES	FULFILLED/VERSES	TOTAL PROPHETIC CONTENT	PERCENTAGE
1/2	7/7	9 VERSES	2%

Nehemiah left his high position as King Artaxerxes's cupbearer for a ministry of restoration in Jerusalem, and Artaxerxes's decree to restore Jerusalem began the official countdown to the arrival of the Messiah in Jerusalem before his crucifixion (Daniel 9:25-27).

The single greatest prophetic detail in the book of Nehemiah is the decree of Artaxerxes to rebuild Jerusalem (Nehemiah 2:1-8). In the sweeping prophecy of Jewish history found in Daniel 9:24-27, Daniel was given an overview of the 490-year period of Jewish history from his day all the way to the end times, excepting the gap of time known as the church age. This all-important prophecy is detailed in the upcoming chapter "The Major Prophets," but the one detail that is specifically associated with the book of Nehemiah and Artaxerxes's decree is found in Daniel 9:25: "Know and understand this: From the time the word goes out to restore and rebuild Jerusalem until the Anointed One, the ruler, comes, there will be seven 'sevens,' and sixty-two 'sevens.'"

This amazing prophecy provided the exact time frame for Jesus's arrival in Jerusalem on Palm Sunday in AD 32. It foretold that there would be 69 sets of seven years, or 483 years on the Jewish calendar, between a call to "rebuild Jerusalem" and the arrival of "the Anointed One."

We know from Nehemiah 2:1 (and well-established historical records) that in 445 BC, King Artaxerxes issued his decree allowing Nehemiah to go and rebuild Jerusalem, beginning with the walls around the city. We are told this happened in the month of Nisan in the twentieth year of Artaxerxes. Long story short, we can identify this exact date based on historical and archaeological records. Fast-forward 483 years (using the Jewish 360-day calendar), and this brings us to the spring of AD 32, the exact time of Jesus's triumphal entry into Jerusalem on Palm Sunday.

Many credible prophecy experts have taken the time to calculate all the dates and study the historical references that back up the specific year identified in Nehemiah 2, and they make an extremely strong case that this prophecy of 483 Jewish years was fulfilled to the exact day!

ESTHER

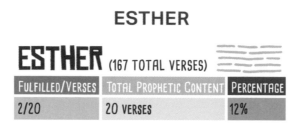

ESTHER (167 TOTAL VERSES)

FULFILLED/VERSES	TOTAL PROPHETIC CONTENT	PERCENTAGE
2/20	20 VERSES	12%

God is not mentioned in the book of Esther, but his sovereignty and divine providence are seen throughout. Esther was willing to risk her life to save others and advocate for them to the king of Persia, and God protected the Jewish people and the line of the Messiah.

Antisemitism is an age-old, satanically inspired evil. God made many specific prophetic promises to the Jewish people that find their ultimate fulfillment at the end of the age. Throughout history, Satan has inspired repeated attempts to completely destroy the Jewish people in the hopes of keeping God's prophetic decrees from coming to pass. We see a powerful case study of this in the book of Esther. Whether it's the Spanish Inquisition, the pogroms of Russia, Nazi Germany, or the many modern-day attacks on Israel, we see this phenomenon arise again and again. We also see God repeatedly preserve the Jewish people in miraculous ways all through the ages.

The common pattern with antisemitism begins in the spiritual realm, with Satan raising up evil rulers over and over who try to destroy the Jewish people (3:6). But those evil rulers are always eventually destroyed (7:9-10), and the opposition causes the Jewish people to band together for survival (9:16). An interesting fact to note is that the holiday of Purim was instituted in Esther chapter 9 and is still celebrated by Jewish people today.

GOD'S SOVEREIGN PLAN CONTINUES

Throughout the historical section of the Old Testament, we get a clear overview of how earthly history progresses within the banks of the river of God's sovereign plan. The progressive revelation of prophecy plays out as it is fulfilled in real time and in real history. Though evil rulers in the seen and unseen realms tried to harm God's people and thwart God's plans, nothing could stop the messianic line of David from remaining intact. Nothing could prevent God's promises from being kept or his prophesies from being fulfilled. All the winding events in the historical section of the Old Testament unflinchingly prepared the way for the Messiah to arrive.

That should give us great confidence that even though we face many trials in life and often don't see how God is going to work out his plans, he will surely accomplish his will in our lives and in world events. God never paces the floor of his throne room wondering what to do next. He is not surprised by the twists and turns of history. All is perfectly aligned with his overarching and unstoppable prophetic will. We are part of a truly amazing story, and we can confidently put our trust in a God who keeps his promises. His track record speaks for itself.

CHAPTER 5

Waxing Prophetically Poetic

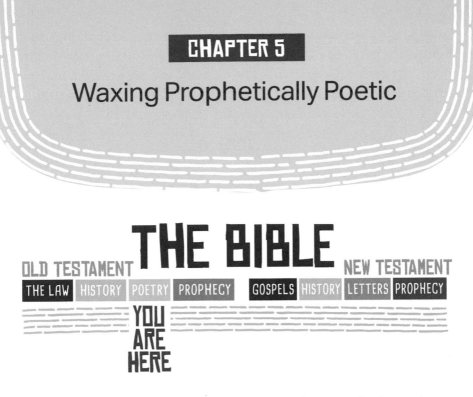

I know that you can do all things; no purpose of yours can be thwarted.

—JOB 42:2

There are some incredible prophetic themes in the section of the Old Testament known as the Poetry books. The expressive and beautifully poetic books of Job, Psalms, Proverbs, Ecclesiastes, and Song of Solomon demonstrate how God used the personalities of the biblical writers to express his truth in many different ways. Though we see the use of poetic literary devices in this part of the Bible, we must not forget that "all Scripture is God-breathed" (2 Timothy 3:16). God is the true author of the Bible; it was he who spoke through the various writers who penned Scripture (2 Peter 1:21).

There is an incredible amount of prophecy found in the Poetry books. For example, in Job we find a passage about a future redeemer and the resurrection of the dead (Job 19:25-27). In the Psalms, messianic prophecies of Christ's first advent and future return as king are woven throughout. In Proverbs, Jesus embodies the characteristics of wisdom. In Ecclesiastes, we're told that in the future, God will "bring every deed into judgment, including every hidden thing, whether it is good or evil" (12:14). Finally, in Song of Solomon, some scholars find typology that foreshadows Christ and the church as his bride.

JOB

JOB (1,070 TOTAL VERSES)

PROPHECIES/VERSES	TYPES	TOTAL PROPHETIC CONTENT	PERCENTAGE
9/36	2/6	42 VERSES	4%

MESSIANIC: 2 (6 VERSES) | END-TIMES PROPHECIES: 1 (3 VERSES)

Though the book of Job is a historical narrative from the early time of the patriarchs, Job knew that a redeemer was coming and that he himself (Job) would be resurrected in a new body and see the Savior with his own eyes. In Job 19:25-27, we read, "I know that my redeemer lives, and that in the end he will stand on the earth. And after my skin has been destroyed, yet in my flesh I will see God; I myself will see him with my own eyes—I, and not another. How my heart yearns within me!"

What a powerfully prophetic statement! Surely, this key truth helped to keep Job moving forward in the midst of his tremendous trials. Job lost his wealth, his children, his health, and his friends. Even Job's wife encouraged him to "curse God and die!" (Job 2:9). But God sustained Job. I believe it is safe to say that God's promises are part of what gave Job hope in the face of terrible pain and loss.

Theologically and prophetically speaking, Job knew and boldly proclaimed that the future Redeemer is God himself (eternal/already living in Job's time), that this world will one day end, that the Redeemer would stand on the earth (see Zechariah 14:4), and that the righteous dead would be resurrected and see God firsthand. All these details line up with prophecies and theological details revealed later in Scripture. The cohesiveness of Scripture is evidence to its single author.

Another amazing fact about the book of Job is that it contains many scientific facts that we now know are true: the earth is suspended/floats in space (26:7), light moves (38:19-20), oceans have deep springs (38:16), water evaporates and condenses in the hydrologic cycle (36:27-28), and there is gravity in space (38:31). Job even mentions dinosaurs (40:15-19; 41). While these facts are not prophetic of the future, they serve as additional powerful evidence that the Creator of all things is the author of the Bible.

PSALMS

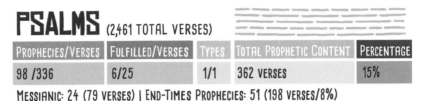

PSALMS (2,461 TOTAL VERSES)				
PROPHECIES/VERSES	FULFILLED/VERSES	TYPES	TOTAL PROPHETIC CONTENT	PERCENTAGE
98 /336	6/25	1/1	362 VERSES	15%

MESSIANIC: 24 (79 VERSES) | END-TIMES PROPHECIES: 51 (198 VERSES/8%)

King David wrote many of the psalms, but there were other authors as well. Those include the sons of Korah, Solomon, Moses (one psalm), and some anonymous writer(s). David is named as the author of 75 of the psalms.

Some of the most famous chapters in the book are Psalm 22, which clearly portrays the events of Jesus's death hundreds of years before it occurred, and Psalm 23, which beautifully depicts God as a caring and wise shepherd. In fact, there are 13 distinctively messianic psalms (2; 8; 16; 22; 40; 45; 69; 72; 89; 102; 109; 110; 132).

In addition to psalms related to the Messiah's first advent, there are also psalms that foretell events connected to his return and the establishment of the millennial kingdom. Psalms 2 and 110 are great examples (see also 22:28; 48:1; 72:8; 102:16; 105:10-11; 132:13-14).

These passages are so clearly detailed that they cannot be explained away as mere allegory. In other words, these prophecies—if taken at face value and understood literally (as they should be), necessarily require a future kingdom age featuring the messianic descendant of David ruling the entire world from Jerusalem in a golden era of righteousness. It also requires the existence of Israel and the Jewish people during this period. These details line up with what God would later reveal in Revelation chapters 12 and 20 (and in many of the books of the prophets, as we will see in upcoming chapters).

Consider these two passages from the Psalms, which demonstrate the permanence of God's commitment to Israel and the Jewish people, and how this will all be fulfilled in a future kingdom age.

Psalm 130:7-8

> Israel, put your hope in the LORD, for with the LORD is *unfailing* love and with him is *full* redemption. He himself will redeem Israel from all their sins.

(Note: Compare that with Romans 11:26, which states that one day, "all Israel will be saved.")

Psalm 132:11-14, 17-18

> The LORD swore an oath to David, a sure oath he will not revoke: "One of your own descendants I will place on your throne. If your sons keep my covenant and the statutes I teach them, then their sons will sit on your throne *for ever and ever*." For the LORD has chosen Zion [Jerusalem], he has desired it for his dwelling, saying, "This is my resting place *for ever and ever*; here I will sit enthroned, for I have desired it…Here I will make a horn [symbol of power/a ruler] grow for David and set up a lamp for my anointed one. I will clothe his enemies with shame, but his head will be adorned with a radiant crown."

PROVERBS

PROVERBS (915 TOTAL VERSES)

PROPHECIES/VERSES	TOTAL PROPHETIC CONTENT	PERCENTAGE
8/10	10 VERSES	1%

Proverbs are, for the most part, general principles of practical wisdom that help people live godly lives. But within the book there are a handful of prophecies as well. In addition to the small number of prophetic texts, there is one key verse that applies to prophecy but is itself more of a principle than a prophecy. Proverbs 29:18 reads, "Where there is no revelation, people cast off restraint; but blessed is the one who heeds wisdom's instruction."

The word "revelation" in this verse literally means "prophetic vision." In other words, if mankind is left with no clear view of God's prophetic future, people will live selfishly and lawlessly. When there is no expectation of future judgment or God's intervention, people cast off all restraint and live any way they desire.

Personally, I think one major reason for apostasy and the broad surface-level cultural Christianity of our day is the lack of prophetic teaching in churches. Without the clear and compelling proclamation of God's prophetic Word, people become removed from a major aspect of Scripture's transformative power. Without a knowledge of Bible prophecy and how it ties the narrative of Scripture together from Genesis to Revelation, many Christians miss out on the exciting expectation of the Lord's soon return.

ECCLESIASTES

ECCLESIASTES (222 TOTAL VERSES)

PROPHECIES/VERSES	TYPES	TOTAL PROPHETIC CONTENT	PERCENTAGE
5/5	1/1	6 VERSES	2%

Solomon's name is not mentioned in the book of Ecclesiastes, but specific details let us know that he was indeed the writer. He was the only one of David's sons who ruled as king over the united nation of Israel. After Solomon, the country split into two kingdoms. As mentioned when we looked at 1 and 2 Kings, Solomon started strong, but then compromised.

In terms of prophecy, there are a few here in Ecclesiastes. Most notable are two verses that proclaim the future judgment of the righteous and the wicked. First, in Ecclesiastes 3:17, we read, "God will bring into judgment both the righteous and the wicked, for there will be a time for every activity, a time to judge every deed."

This theme is repeated at the end of the book as well, in the very last verse of Ecclesiastes: "God will bring every deed into judgment, including every hidden thing, whether it is good or evil" (12:14).

We discover the full picture of God's future judgments later in the New Testament, where we read about the bema seat judgment (the judgment seat of Christ) for Christians (see Romans 14:10-12 and 2 Corinthians 5:10) and the great white throne judgment for the unrighteous (see Revelation 20:11-15).

SONG OF SOLOMON

SONG OF SOLOMON (117 TOTAL VERSES)

TOTAL PROPHETIC CONTENT	PERCENTAGE	NOT CITED ANYWHERE IN THE NEW TESTAMENT AS TYPOLOGY, BUT THERE ARE SOME COMPELLING DETAILS THAT COULD VERY WELL BE TYPOLOGY.
0 VERSES	0%	

The Song of Solomon does not have any overt prophecies or explicit types that are noted elsewhere in Scripture. There are some verses that could be typological references in which Solomon and his wife point to Christ and the church. But this is somewhat speculative, and because there are no specific verses in the New Testament that explicitly identify these supposed types as such, I am reluctant to cite them here as typology. Personally, I believe there are some types within the Song of Solomon (using the five minimum criteria I cited in chapter 1). But because the New Testament does not specifically indicate any types (the sixth criterion cited in chapter 1) from the Song of Solomon—and because this is a subjective matter—I chose not to include any possible types from the Song of Solomon as prophetic content here.

A GOD WE CAN TRUST

As we consider the fact that the Bible was written by at least 39 different authors over a period of 1,500 years in three different languages and on three different continents, it is absolutely amazing to think that this collection of 66 books could be cohesive on any level. Yet here—even in the books of poetry—we discover the consistent unifying features of given prophecies and fulfilled prophecies.

From the earliest writings in the book of Job to the beautiful prose in the Psalms, we see the hallmarks of the Redeemer progressively revealed over time. What an awe-inspiring God we serve! He alone can capture the human heart with words creatively assembled and, at the same time, assure us the passages are from a divine source—as proven through the incredible apologetic of fulfilled prophecy.

This is yet another affirmation of the hope that is ours because we can trust God's future promises, which are backed up by the impeccable track record of the poetic Promise-Keeper.

CHAPTER 6

The Incredible Prophecies of Isaiah

THE BIBLE

OLD TESTAMENT | NEW TESTAMENT

THE LAW | HISTORY | POETRY | PROPHECY | GOSPELS | HISTORY | LETTERS | PROPHECY

YOU ARE HERE

*Surely he took up our pain and bore our suffering,
yet we considered him punished by God, stricken by him, and afflicted.
But he was pierced for our transgressions, he was crushed for our iniquities;
the punishment that brought us peace was on
him, and by his wounds we are healed.*

—ISAIAH 53:4-5

ISAIAH (1,292 TOTAL VERSES)

PROPHECIES/VERSES	FULFILLED/VERSES	TOTAL PROPHETIC CONTENT	PERCENTAGE
107/751	7/14	765 VERSES	59%

MESSIANIC: 6 (40 VERSES) | END-TIMES PROPHECIES: 23 (195 VERSES)

Whenever I have the opportunity to go to the movies, I don't like to be late. Some people skip the sneak previews, but to me, they are a vital part of the movie-going experience. Sneak previews are exciting because they are like mini-movies that feature the best parts. They are designed to whet your appetite so that when the full movie comes out, you'll grab a few friends or family members and pay your hard-earned money to sit in a darkened theater for a couple of hours to take it all in.

In many ways, prophecies are like sneak previews. They don't give us every detail, but they hit the high points and make us look forward to the day when they are fulfilled. Many prophecies given in Scripture (particularly here in the prophetic books of the Old Testament) serve as highlight reels of coming future events. Earlier in chapter 4, I mentioned this when we discussed the mountain peaks of prophecy and how details in a single verse or prophetic section can be separated by hundreds or even thousands of years. Often the prophets would give a detailed prophecy with an immediate context, then, without warning, switch gears and proclaim a prophecy about the end times.

Aside from the amazing fulfilled and yet-future prophesies found in Isaiah, there's another very interesting fact about the book: It has 66 chapters. The first 39 make up one section, which is mostly about denunciation and coming judgment. The second section is made up of 27 chapters that focus primarily on grace and restoration. Scholars have pointed out how this mirrors the composition of the Bible itself, which has 39 Old Testament books that point to the need for a Savior, and 27 New Testament books that record his ministry of reconciliation/restoration and the outworking of God's grace.

Key second-coming sections in the last 27 chapters of Isaiah include several portions foretelling of a future golden kingdom age with a descendant of King David (Jesus) ruling in a world that looks much different than ours today, but is not yet heaven or the eternal state. Similar prophecies are found in Ezekiel, the Psalms, and other books in the prophetic section of the

Old Testament. We learn more details about the duration and chronology of this future golden age—during which righteousness rules the entire world—in the last book of the Bible. Revelation chapter 20 states six times that this future kingdom will be 1,000 years in duration. All the passages about this age speak in literal terms, so there is no reason to allegorize the many descriptions. These prophecies make sense only if there will be a literal worldwide kingdom on earth ruled by the Messiah.

With that in mind, let's look at a few key sections of prophecy from the book of Isaiah. As you can imagine, based on the significant percentage of prophecy found in Isaiah (as indicated in the chart on page 81), it was hard to decide what to focus on. So I have tried to present some of the most compelling passages, and I've listed them chronologically, in the order that they appear in Isaiah.

CHRISTMAS CONUNDRUM

Isaiah 9:6 is quoted frequently at Christmastime. You may have seen the passage on Christmas cards, oftentimes along with a manger scene. The well-known (but usually not fully understood) verse reads, "To us a child is born, to us a son is given, and the government will be on his shoulders. And he will be called Wonderful Counselor, Mighty God, Everlasting Father, Prince of Peace."

Notice that the first three phrases correlate to three distinct events in the ministry of Jesus, each separated by time. First, he was born. Then 33 years later, the Son of God was given as a sacrifice for sin (John 3:16). Then one day yet future, the government will be on his shoulders. He will reign over all the nations of earth during the millennial kingdom as the Prince of Peace.

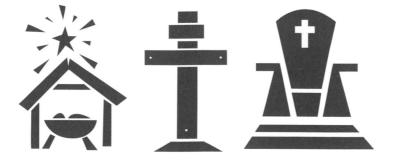

Isaiah 9:7 continues the kingdom theme, saying, "Of the greatness of his government and peace there will be no end. He will reign on David's throne and over his kingdom, establishing and upholding it with justice and righteousness from that time on and forever. The zeal of the LORD Almighty will accomplish this."

Other notable messianic passages include Isaiah 11:1-2 and the incredibly detailed prophecies in Isaiah 53 (see page 89).

THE ESCHATOLOGY OF ISAIAH

One of the key themes woven throughout the Old Testament prophetic books is a future time of judgment and restoration known as the Day of the Lord. This day can refer to any time God intervenes in history to judge a nation. The term is also used to describe the events surrounding the end times—particularly the future tribulation period (Isaiah 2:12-19; 4:1), the return of Christ (Joel 2:30-32), and the subsequent millennial kingdom (Isaiah 4:2; 12; 19:23-25; Jeremiah 30:7-9).

When the Day of the Lord is used in an eschatological (end-times) sense, it can mean any or all three of those aspects. Context determines which aspect is being spoken of. Sometimes, as with the prophet Joel, the text details the tribulation-period events only, whereas in other passages we see a back-and-forth foretelling of both the tribulation period and the millennial kingdom—sometimes in chronological order and sometimes not. Most often, the Day of the Lord is referring to the future time when the Lord will return to judge the world then set up his literal, prophesied kingdom on earth.

We aren't told the duration of the tribulation period until Daniel 9. And we aren't told the duration of the millennial kingdom until Revelation 20. But the definitive prediction that the world will experience a global time of God's judgment followed by a golden era during which the Messiah will rule the world is seen throughout the books of the prophets. These key future events are highlighted with progressive clarity throughout the books of the prophets, beginning with the book of Isaiah.

We see both components clearly detailed in Isaiah chapter 2. In verses 9-21 we come to the first passage in Isaiah regarding the time of future judgment. And in verses 2-4, we see a clear snapshot of the subsequent kingdom age.

The Tribulation Period

Consider these select verses from Isaiah chapter 2:

> People will be brought low and everyone humbled—do not forgive them. Go into the rocks, hide in the ground from the fearful presence of the LORD and the splendor of his majesty! The eyes of the arrogant will be humbled and human pride brought low; the LORD alone will be exalted in that day. The Lord Almighty has a day in store for all the proud and lofty, for all that is exalted (and they will be humbled) (verses 9-12).

> The arrogance of man will be brought low and human pride humbled; the LORD alone will be exalted in that day (verse 17).

> People will flee to caves in the rocks and to holes in the ground from the fearful presence of the LORD and the splendor of his majesty, when he rises to shake the earth (verse 19).

> They will flee to caverns in the rocks and to the overhanging crags from the fearful presence of the LORD and the splendor of his majesty, when he rises to shake the earth (verse 21).

Now compare those passages with Revelation 6:15-17, which reads,

> The kings of the earth, the princes, the generals, the rich, the mighty, and everyone else, both slave and free, hid in caves and among the rocks of the mountains. They called to the mountains and the rocks, "Fall on us and hide us from the face of him who sits on the throne and from the wrath of the Lamb! For the great day of their wrath has come, and who can withstand it?"

God has an appointed time—"a day in store"—to humble the proud and godless rulers of the world. He will rise and "shake the earth." Isaiah 2 and Revelation 6 (toward the end of the first set of judgments during the tribulation) detail the moment when these future elite movers and shakers will realize that they are experiencing the active wrath of God.

Here is a select list of other passages in Isaiah that refer to the tribulation period: 11:4-5; 13:6-13; 17:4-9.

The Millennial Kingdom

The future tribulation period (which we will examine more fully in upcoming chapters, particularly when we get to the books of Daniel and Revelation) will be followed by the kingdom age, which Isaiah 2:2-4 describes in this way:

> In the last days the mountain of the LORD's temple will be established as the highest of the mountains; it will be exalted above the hills, and all nations will stream to it. Many peoples will come and say, "Come, let us go up to the mountain of the LORD, to the temple of the God of Jacob. He will teach us his ways, so that we may walk in his paths." The law will go out from Zion, the word of the LORD from Jerusalem. He will judge between the nations and will settle disputes for many peoples. They will beat their swords into plowshares and their spears into pruning hooks. Nation will not take up sword against nation, nor will they train for war anymore.

Notice that the topography will be transformed, the future temple in Jerusalem will be the highest spot on earth, Jesus himself will rule and teach from Jerusalem (Zion), he will settle disputes between people, and there will be no war at all during Christ's reign! We learn from Isaiah 11:6-9 that the animal kingdom will be dramatically changed as well. There will be no carnivorous, poisonous, or dangerous animals. The earth will return to an Edenic state (more on this and the purposes and duration of the kingdom age in chapter 14, where we will explore the book of Revelation).

Here is a select list of other passages in Isaiah that refer to the millennial kingdom: 11:6-10; 12:1-6; 18:7; 19:16-25; 55:3-5; 56:1-2, 5-8; 58:11-12; 59:17-21; 60:1-22; 61:3-11; 62:1-12; 64:17-24.

Isaiah's Little Apocalypse

If the brief lists of verses I included above regarding the tribulation period and the future kingdom age intrigue you, you may want to pause here and take some time to read four full chapters of Isaiah. We see these end-times themes repeated throughout Isaiah, but nowhere are they more prominent than in chapters 24–27, which are commonly referred to as Isaiah's little apocalypse.

This portion of the book follows a very long section (chapters 13–23) on the judgment of specific Gentile nations. In Isaiah's little apocalypse, the focus shifts from the judgment of individual nations to an end-times judgment of the entire earth, which has not happened yet. This pattern of near-fulfillment predictions interspersed with clear end-times worldwide predictions of judgment is also found in most of the other Old Testament prophetic books as well.

When you carefully compare passages such as Isaiah's little apocalypse (and Jeremiah has a similar passage, as we'll see in the next chapter) with the book of Revelation and Jesus's Olivet Discourse in Matthew 24–25 (as well as key passages in the other Old Testament prophetic books), the details complement, support, and enhance one another to give us a more complete picture of end-times events. Again, if you have time, I recommend pausing here and reading Isaiah chapters 24–27 in their entirety.

THE DOOM OF DAMASCUS

In Isaiah 17 is a prophecy about the sudden and complete destruction of the ancient city of Damascus. We're not told exactly when this will occur, but many prophecy experts believe it will happen prior to the Ezekiel 38 war. This makes sense given what we see happening in Syria today. Isaiah 17:1 says, "See, Damascus will no longer be a city but will become a heap of ruins." Verse 14 adds, "At evening time, behold, there is terror! Before morning they are gone. This will be the fate of those who plunder us and the lot of those who pillage us" (NASB). The phrase "in that day" is sprinkled throughout Isaiah 17, and many prophecy experts note that this phrase is often associated with the end times (that is, the Day of the Lord).

Damascus is the oldest continually inhabited city in existence. Many prophecy experts think that the sudden destruction of Damascus will be the catalyst that triggers the Ezekiel 38 war, or that will occur in conjunction with the Ezekiel 38 war. These 2,600-year-old prophecies have not been fulfilled as of yet. Damascus, though ravaged by the Syrian civil war, still stands and still has people living there (perhaps Jeremiah 49:23-27 is occurring in our day as a lead-up to the full destruction of Damascus). As we've seen recently in the news, there are several Russian, Iranian, and Syrian military installations in and around Damascus, as well as the presence of chemical weapons and the headquarters of several terrorist groups that are proxies of Iran.

Iran is setting up shop in Damascus and openly states its religiously driven plans to destroy Israel. Airstrikes from 2017 right up to the present time performed by the Israeli military against weapons convoys and Iranian installments near Damascus makes one wonder how close we are to Isaiah 17 (and Ezekiel 38, which we'll discuss in chapter 8). We're not told who destroys Damascus or how, but the surrounding verses suggest it's during a conflict with Israel. Recent events indicate this could take place as a preemptive strike by Israel in order to ensure the Jewish nation's survival. This could be a nuclear strike or a conventional strike that triggers such widespread destruction that the city is wiped out overnight (see Isaiah 17:1, 14; Jeremiah 49:23-27).

If you have viewed media footage of the 2020 explosion in Beirut, it is not difficult to imagine how the prophecy in Isaiah 17 could happen in our day. Many prophecy experts believe this event could occur immediately prior to or right after the rapture, and say that the Ezekiel 38 war may happen in conjunction with or as a result of the fulfillment of Isaiah 17.

INCREDIBLY INTRIGUING ISAIAH 53

Isaiah 53 clearly depicts Jesus's suffering and death on the cross 700 years before it happened. Critics used to attempt to place the writings of Isaiah after first-century AD events because Isaiah 53 so clearly describes many details about the suffering of the Messiah. They didn't believe it was possible for anyone to so accurately portray the crucifixion. But, in 1947 (and following), the Dead Sea Scrolls were discovered, including the Isaiah Scroll, which dates to the second century BC. The Dead Sea Scrolls were copies of long-established religious texts that belonged to the Qumran community, and this evidence that Isaiah was written long before the time of Christ confirms the book's truly amazing prophetic nature.

If you are familiar with the details of the Gospels—particularly their record of Christ's trials, death, burial, and resurrection, you may want to pause here and read all of Isaiah 53. It very clearly predicted the substitutionary nature of Christ's death, his sinlessness, his trials, his rejection and abandonment by the people, the nature of his death (being pierced), and specific details about his burial, resurrection, and future victorious reign!

Here are a few select verses from Isaiah 53 to ponder:

> He was pierced for our transgressions, he was crushed for our iniquities; the punishment that brought us peace was on him, and by his wounds we are healed (verse 5).

> We all, like sheep, have gone astray,

each of us has turned to our own way; and the LORD has laid on him the iniquity of us all (verse 6).

He was oppressed and afflicted, yet he did not open his mouth; he was led like a lamb to the slaughter, and as a sheep before its shearers is silent, so he did not open his mouth (verse 7).

By oppression and judgment he was taken away. Yet who of his generation protested? For he was cut off from the land of the living; for the transgression of my people he was punished (verse 8).

He was assigned a grave with the wicked, and with the rich in his death, though he had done no violence, nor was any deceit in his mouth (verse 9).

Yet it was the LORD's will to crush him and cause him to suffer, and though the LORD makes his life an offering for sin, he will see his offspring and prolong his days, and the will of the LORD will prosper in his hand (verse 10).

After he has suffered, he will see the light of life and be satisfied; by his knowledge my righteous servant will justify many, and he will bear their iniquities (verse 11).

Therefore I will give him a portion among the great, and he will divide the spoils with the strong, because he poured out his life unto death, and was numbered with the transgressors. For he bore the sins of many, and made intercession for the transgressors (verse 12).

If you had not known these verses were from the book of Isaiah, written more than 700 years before the ministry of Jesus, you would think you were reading an account of the death and resurrection of Christ from one of the Gospels! Every single detail in those verses can be synced with the specifics of what happened at the cross.

ISRAEL BORN IN A DAY

Isaiah 66 provides a poetic panoramic view of Israel's future glory. Sprinkled through the text are vignettes of the tribulation period (verses 6, 16), mentions of the kingdom age, and intriguing words about Israel being reborn in a day and brought forth in a moment (verse 8).

BIRTH CERTIFICATE

NAME: ISRAEL

DATE: MAY 14, 1948

In Isaiah 66:8, we read, "Who has ever heard of such things? Who has ever seen things like this? Can a country be born in a day or a nation be brought forth in a moment? Yet no sooner is Zion in labor than she gives birth to her children." Many prophecy experts have noted that in fulfillment of this prophecy, the nation of Israel was literally born in a day on May 14, 1948. Every Old Testament prophet except for Jonah predicted that Israel would become a nation again. This mind-blowing fulfillment came to pass in our modern era.

UNDERSTANDING GOD'S PLAN FOR THE AGES

The incredible prophecies in Isaiah about the first coming, the tribulation period, and the millennial kingdom should get our attention. As highlighted earlier in this chapter, many believers understand the importance of Isaiah 9:6 at Christmastime but fail to interpret literally what Isaiah 9:7 says about a future kingdom in which the government of the entire world will be on the Messiah's shoulders. This twofold pairing of prophecies occurs in the book of Isaiah as well as in other prophetic books. Getting a clear comprehension of the twofold prophecies related to the first and second advents of Jesus are key to understanding God's plan for the ages.

CHAPTER 7

Prophecies from the Weeping Prophet

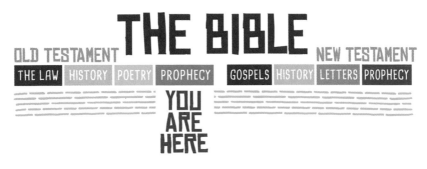

THE BIBLE

OLD TESTAMENT | NEW TESTAMENT

THE LAW | HISTORY | POETRY | PROPHECY | GOSPELS | HISTORY | LETTERS | PROPHECY

YOU ARE HERE

Before I formed you in the womb I knew you, before you were born I set you apart; I appointed you as a prophet to the nations.

—JEREMIAH 1:5

"The days are coming," declares the LORD, "when I will bring my people Israel and Judah back from captivity and restore them to the land I gave their ancestors to possess," says the LORD.

—JEREMIAH 30:3

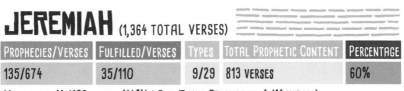

JEREMIAH (1,364 TOTAL VERSES)

PROPHECIES/VERSES	FULFILLED/VERSES	TYPES	TOTAL PROPHETIC CONTENT	PERCENTAGE
135/674	35/110	9/29	813 VERSES	60%

MESSIANIC: 11 (186 VERSES/14%) | END-TIMES PROPHECIES: 1 (11 VERSES)

Jeremiah is known as the weeping prophet. His 42-year ministry to the southern kingdom of Judah was a tough assignment. Jeremiah had the difficult job of calling the rulers and people to repentance and warning them of impending judgment if they refused to return to God. Through the reigns of kings Josiah, Jehoahaz, Jehoiakin, Jehoiachin, and Zedekiah, Jeremiah's pleas fell on spiritually deaf ears. The prophet was rejected, beaten, imprisoned, thrown into a deep empty well (and later rescued), and endured many other hardships during his long, lonely ministry. Chief among them was witnessing the fulfillment of his prophecies of Judah being conquered and taken captive by the Babylonians. After the Babylonian attack on Judah and Jerusalem, Jeremiah was freed, then taken to Egypt.

In terms of prophetic content, we see the similar pattern of a prophet of God warning the people of his day about God's near judgment—then shifting without warning to forecast the much-greater reality of global judgment in the last days. Jeremiah is similar to Isaiah in that his book contains lengthy, detailed depictions of end-times events related to the future tribulation period and the kingdom age. We'll look at some such passages, but first, there is an important prophecy I would like to draw your attention to because it was fulfilled in our era, and Jeremiah mentions it prominently twice.

BIGGER THAN THE EXODUS

When we read about the incredible wonders that God performed through Moses with the ten plagues of Egypt and the miraculous parting of the Red Sea, we're left with a sense of awe and amazement. These events actually happened! Movies have been made about the plagues and the Red Sea, and thousands of years later, believers all over the world still tell the stories of what took place.

In the book of Jeremiah, we're told on two different occasions that a miracle greater than the exodus was to occur. Even more riveting is the fact that this miraculous prophecy has been fulfilled in modern times! Under the inspiration of the Holy Spirit, Jeremiah proclaims twice that the rebirth of the nation of Israel would be a greater miracle than the events surrounding the exodus and the parting of the Red Sea. I've included both passages for you below.

Jeremiah 16:14-15

"However, the days are coming," declares the LORD, "when it will no longer be said, 'As surely as the LORD lives, who brought the Israelites up out of Egypt,' but it will be said, 'As surely as the LORD lives, who brought the Israelites up out of the land of the north and out of all the countries where he had banished them.' For I will restore them to the land I gave their ancestors."

Jeremiah 23:7-8

"The days are coming," declares the LORD, "when people will no longer say, 'As surely as the LORD lives, who brought the Israelites up out of Egypt,' but they will say, 'As surely as the LORD lives, who brought the descendants of Israel up out of the land of the north and out of all the countries where he had banished them.' Then they will live in their own land."

When you consider the millions of details that had to come together in order for the Jewish people to return to their homeland after 1,878 years of being scattered and mistreated all over the world, you can see why Jeremiah considered this single event to be more miraculous and momentous than the parting of the Red Sea. In preparation for all the dramatic end-times events that will take place in the future, Israel had to be in existence once again—and this incredible prophecy was fulfilled in our modern era. These are biblical times! (See also Jeremiah 32:37-38.)

THE ESCHATOLOGY OF JEREMIAH

With the all-important prophecy of Israel's rebirth fulfilled, the stage is set for the other end-times events prophesied by Jeremiah to take place. As mentioned above, Jeremiah had quite a bit to say about the tribulation period and the future kingdom age. For example, there is a densely packed passage about the tribulation years in in Jeremiah 4:23-28, where we read,

I looked at the earth, and it was formless and empty; and at the heavens, and their light was gone. I looked at the mountains, and they were quaking; all the hills were swaying. I looked, and there were no people; every bird in the sky had flown away. I looked, and the fruitful land was a desert; all its towns lay in ruins before the LORD, before his fierce anger. This is what the LORD says: "The whole land will be ruined, though I will not destroy it completely. Therefore the earth will mourn and the heavens above grow dark, because I have spoken and will not relent, I have decided and will not turn back."

If this scene were a painting, it would show a wide-angle shot of the earth's landscape having been decimated by the 21 judgments we read about in the book of Revelation. The earth will be so laid bare from the destruction that it will be almost as formless and void as the earth was before the days of creation. Indeed, the similarity will be so great that God will have to renovate the world in order to usher in the beauty of the kingdom age that follows the tribulation.

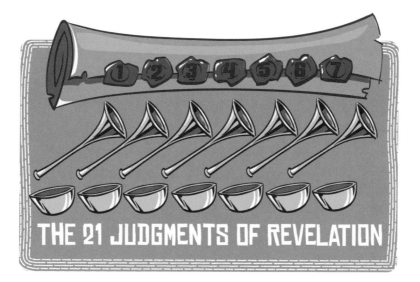

THE 21 JUDGMENTS OF REVELATION

This may be a good place to mention that there are different types of judgment. For example, in Romans chapter 1 (which we'll highlight in chapter 12), we learn about God's abandonment wrath—where he steps back to allow a people to get their wishes and live with the consequences of kicking God out of their culture and decisions. Any nation in history that knows God's revealed truth then pushes God out of its dealings will experience his abandonment wrath. It is a fixed spiritual law. Sadly, we've witnessed this very trajectory in the US the past several decades—and we are experiencing God's abandonment wrath. Thankfully, in the midst of this, God cares for his own and promises never to abandon his children.

Then here in the prophetic books (and in the book of Revelation) we learn about God's active and intentional wrath upon the nations of the earth via the Day of the Lord or tribulation period. There is also a lesser-known judgment found in Scripture known as the sheep and goats judgment. In this future judgment, the Gentile nations will be judged over how they will have treated Israel during the tribulation period. (We'll discuss this more at length in chapter 11.) Finally, we learn about the ultimate judgment known as the great white throne judgment in Revelation 19, which is a final, eternal, and spiritual judgment that will take place at the end of time.

Jeremiah 25—Jeremiah's Little Apocalypse

One reason people are so intimidated by the book of Revelation is that they see it as a stand-alone book that is somewhat disconnected from the rest of Scripture, but this could not be further from the truth. As we study Scripture systematically, we discover several other key sections in it that help explain the same future time period. As we saw in the previous chapter, Isaiah has a section that can be described as a little apocalypse. Here in Jeremiah, we find a similar passage delivered to us by the prophet. I would encourage you to pause here and read the full text of Jeremiah 25 before continuing onward.

The first 14 verses talk about the immediate context of Jeremiah's day—the coming 70-year captivity of God's people. But verses 15-38 look to the future end-times tribulation period. Verse 15 makes this clear, saying, "This is what the LORD, the God of Israel, said to me: 'Take from my hand this cup filled with the wine of my wrath and make all the nations to whom I send you drink it.'" Then in verse 26, we see that the judgment Jeremiah is describing concerns "all the kingdoms on the face of the earth." Then again in verse 29, we read, "I am calling down a sword on all who live on the earth, declares the LORD Almighty."

Verses 31-33 continue,

"The tumult will resound to the ends of the earth, for the Lord will bring charges against the nations; he will bring judgment on all mankind and put the wicked to the sword," declares the Lord. This is what the Lord Almighty says: "Look! Disaster is spreading from nation to nation; a mighty storm is rising from the ends of the earth."

At that time, those slain by the Lord will be everywhere—from one end of the earth to the other. They will not be mourned or gathered up or buried, but will be left lying on the ground.

Then in the final verse, we read a powerful statement about Jesus, who is "the Lion of the tribe of Judah" (Revelation 5:5; see also Genesis 49:9). Jeremiah says, "Like a lion he will leave his lair, and their land will become desolate because of the sword of the oppressor and because of the Lord's fierce anger" (verse 38).

This is clearly the same time period we read about in Revelation 6, where the Lion begins to judge the earth during the future seven-year tribulation.

Chronology Matters

While many prophetic passages found in the prophetic books of the Old Testament move back and forth between time frames and don't always give us insight into the chronology of events, there are a few sections that demonstrate a clear order of events. One of those sections is found in Jeremiah chapter 30. Here is an outline of the chronology, which lines up with the chronology that we find throughout other prophetic sections of the Bible.

1. Regathering of the Jewish people to their ancient homeland (verse 3)

2. Tribulation period (verses 5-7)

3. Great tribulation/Jacob's trouble (second half of tribulation period) (verse 7)

4. Millennial kingdom (verses 8-9)

Then in verses 10-24, the chapter pulls back to a broader view to provide a more detailed recap of the dispersion of the Jewish people, their regathering, the future kingdom age, the Gog/Magog war (which we'll look at in the next chapter), the tribulation, and the great tribulation. First, Jeremiah provides us with a general chronology, then we are given more commentary about various specific events in that chronology.

THE PERMANENCE OF GOD'S PLANS FOR HIS PEOPLE

In Jeremiah chapters 31 and 33, we are given further insight into God's plans for the Jewish people and his unconditional plans related to them in the end times. By now, you see that this is a key theme that keeps popping up in the Old Testament.

Jeremiah 31 beautifully captures the fact that one day, the full remnant of Israel will finally see Jesus was indeed their Messiah. Paul unpacks this fact from a New Testament perspective in Romans chapters 9–11, but we find the foundation for all of that here in Jeremiah 31. In verses 31-33, we read,

> "The days are coming," declares the LORD, "when I will make a new covenant with the people of Israel and with the people of Judah. It will not be like the covenant I made with their ancestors when I took them by the hand to lead them out of Egypt, because they broke my covenant, though I was a husband to them," declares the LORD. "This is the covenant I will make with the people of Israel after that time," declares the LORD. "I will put my law in their minds and write it on their hearts. I will be their God, and they will be my people."

Then in Jeremiah 33:14-17, we learn that there will be a break in the action, eventually. "David will never fail to have a man to sit on the throne of Israel" (verse 17). This confirms that, in the future, Israel must be in existence, with a descendant of David (Jesus) ruling from Israel.

Lest we still wonder if God's plans for Israel and the Jewish people have gone by the wayside, we're given the crystal-clear proclamation in Jeremiah 33:19-26 that as long as there is day and night—as long as the sun and moon exist—the Davidic covenant will remain.

In Jeremiah 33:20-21, we read,

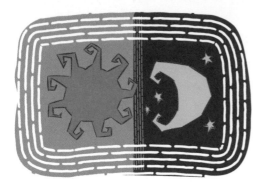

This is what the LORD says: "If you can break my covenant with the day and my covenant with the night, so that day and night no longer come at their appointed time, then my covenant with David my servant—and my covenant with the Levites who are priests ministering before me—can be broken and David will no longer have a descendant to reign on his throne."

Then in verses 25-26, God doubles down on this promise:

This is what the LORD says: "If I have not made my covenant with day and night and established the laws of heaven and earth, then I will reject the descendants of Jacob and David my servant and will not choose one of his sons to rule over the descendants of Abraham, Isaac and Jacob. For I will restore their fortunes and have compassion on them."

These clear proclamations (and many others) confirm that God's promises to Israel will never change and can only be fulfilled in a literal future kingdom age.

A TALE OF TWO CITIES— JERUSALEM AND BABYLON

If you want to trace good and evil in the Bible, just follow the histories of Jerusalem and Babylon. Jerusalem is called the city of God. Babylon, on the other hand, has a rebellious and evil beginning and this theme carries through all of Scripture—culminating in Revelation 17–18, where we read about its future and permanent destruction. Babylon is both a place and a system, similar to how we refer to Wall Street as both a literal location and a financial system.

Babylon shows up in two key forms in the Old Testament: First, in a man-centered, God-defying religious form as seen in the account of Nimrod and the Tower of Babel (Genesis 11). And second, around 1,650 years later, we read about Babylon again, this time in a wealthy, conquering, political form under Nebuchadnezzar. We'll discuss Babylon more in chapter 9, but I highlight it here because the Babylonians were the enemies who conquered Jerusalem during Jeremiah's ministry.

Key passages about Babylon are found in Daniel (which we'll discuss in chapter 9), Isaiah chapters 13, 46–48; Jeremiah 50–51; and Revelation 17–18. You can also read about the record of Babylon invading Judah to destroy Jerusalem and the temple in 2 Kings chapters 17–25 as well as 2 Chronicles chapters 32–36.

In Jeremiah chapters 50–51, we find some of the most extensive prophecies about Babylon, including both near and far fulfillments related to the immediate context as well as the judgment and destruction of Babylon in the end times. We'll discuss this aspect of prophecy in more detail in chapters 9 (Daniel) and 14 (Revelation) of this book.

LAMENTATIONS— POEMS REGARDING JUDGMENT

LAMENTATIONS (154 TOTAL VERSES)			
PROPHECIES/VERSES	FULFILLED/VERSES	TOTAL PROPHETIC CONTENT	PERCENTAGE
1/2	4/82	84 VERSES	54%

This short book includes five poems (one for each chapter) and uses the 22 letters of the Hebrew alphabet at the start of the verses—with the exception of the middle chapter, or chapter 3, which has 66 verses (three per Hebrew letter).

A large percentage of the prophetic content in Lamentations comes in the form of fulfilled prophecy. We read the heartbreaking words of the prophet Jeremiah as he laments and mourns over the destruction of his beloved homeland. Jeremiah's lifetime of

prophetic ministry included faithfully warning the people that judgment was coming, and his firsthand witness of the judgment occurring.

An important lesson we can learn from Jeremiah's tough assignment is this: We are called to serve God faithfully regardless of the outcome. By the world's standards, Jeremiah's ministry was a failure in the sense that nobody listened to his lifelong cries of warning. Yet he remained faithful to God's calling and left the results up to him. Perhaps you are in a tough season of life where you wonder whether what you are doing is making a difference. Jeremiah's life serves as a reminder that our primary responsibility to the Lord is consistent faithfulness—regardless of how others respond.

Although Jeremiah's warnings were not heeded by the leaders of his day, his prophecies are part of God's eternal Word and his example has encouraged many generations toward faithful service to the Lord.

THE BIBLE

OLD TESTAMENT | NEW TESTAMENT

THE LAW | HISTORY | POETRY | PROPHECY | GOSPELS | HISTORY | LETTERS | PROPHECY

YOU ARE HERE

It is not for your sake, people of Israel, that I am going to do these things, but for the sake of my holy name, which you have profaned among the nations where you have gone. I will show the holiness of my great name, which has been profaned among the nations, the name you have profaned among them. Then the nations will know that I am the LORD, declares the Sovereign LORD, when I am proved holy through you before their eyes. For I will take you out of the nations; I will gather you from all the countries and bring you back into your own land.

—EZEKIEL 36:22-24

EZEKIEL (1,273 TOTAL VERSES)

Prophecies/Verses	Fulfilled/Verses	Total Prophetic Content	Percentage
65/832	16/21	853 verses	67%

Messianic: 2 (2 verses) | End-Times Prophecies: 11 (361 verses/28%)

E zekiel is one of the most highly prophetic books in the Bible. It has the largest percentage of prophecy of all the books by the major prophets. The 67 percent of predictive material in Ezekiel is split between

near-fulfillment events of his day (the attack on Jerusalem by Nebuchadnezzar and the Babylonians), and some distant-fulfillment events during the end
times and the future kingdom age. Chapters 1–24 were written before the fall
of Jerusalem, and chapters 33–48 all contain prophecies related to the end
times—beginning with the rebirth of the nation of Israel!

Like Jeremiah, Ezekiel prophesied of coming events, lived through the
fulfillment of those events (he was even taken captive to Babylon), and was
given some amazing prophecies about the last days. Some of these end-times
prophecies—which I'll detail below—have major stage-setting implications
for our day!

EZEKIEL'S EPIC EVIDENCE

In terms of fulfilled prophecies that serve as compelling apologetic
evidence of the divine nature of Scripture, Ezekiel (like the other prophets) includes messianic prophecies (17:22-24; 21:26-27; 34:23-24), as well
as prophecies about the judgment of various nations (25:1–32:32). These
prophecies all came to pass in history exactly as foretold. Some of the most
remarkable examples of fulfillment relate to God's judgments against Philis-
tia (25:15-17) and Tyre (chapters 26:1–28:19).

The Philistines were a constant thorn in the side of Israel. If you'll recall,
the story of David and Goliath featured the Philistine army.

Ezekiel was written in the sixth century BC, and
the Dead Sea Scrolls that were discovered beginning in 1947 confirm
that by 200 BC, the Old Testament Scriptures were already well-
established religious texts. I mention
that because Ezekiel's prophecies
were so specific and so clearly fulfilled
that critics used to say the book had
to have been written after the fact.

The complete destruction of the Philistines was prophesied in Ezekiel 25. Verse
16 said they would be "cut off" (NKJV). This was an Old Testament way of
saying they would no longer be a people group—they would be completely

destroyed. This was fulfilled in the second century BC, four centuries after Ezekiel's prediction. Today, there are no Philistines, but the people of Israel still exist—just as foretold.

Tyre was comprised of a city on the mainland and an island just off the coast. Alexander the Great (of Greece) attacked the island for six months and finally took it by scraping debris from the mainland into the water to build a causeway. The city was later rebuilt, then almost completely destroyed by Muslim invaders in AD 1291. The city has never been rebuilt and—as predicted—fishermen use the scraped and barren area to spread their nets.

This prophecy is so detailed that it takes three chapters to describe, and every aspect was fulfilled perfectly, with all of the details falling into place over a period of several centuries. It is one of the most compelling examples of fulfilled prophecy in the book of Ezekiel. Who but God could have predicted such things so accurately? Again, fulfilled prophecy serves as powerful evidence that the Bible is from God.

OUR FRONT-ROW SEAT TO FULFILLED PROPHECY

Many believers do not realize we currently live in sort of a transition period during which we are witnessing the stage being set for all the end-time drama to unfold. We've seen that there are many Old Testament prophecies regarding Israel's rebirth as a nation in preparation for last-days events. Ezekiel chapters 36–48 serve as a chronological template of those days.

Chapter 36 provides a broad overview that includes the dispersion of the Jewish people (verse 3), the antisemitism and mistreatment the people would endure (verse 3), the land and cities that would lie desolate (verse 4), the fact that the Middle East would remain a geopolitical mess (verse 7), that the Jewish people would eventually return (verse 8), that the land would come back to life and the towns would be rebuilt as the Jewish people continue to multiply in the land (verses 9-10), and that Israel would be more prosperous than in its ancient form (verse 11). Today, Israel—though small enough to fit in Lake Michigan with room to spare—is the eighth most powerful nation in the world. All of this fulfillment has occurred in modern times, beginning with the rebirth of Israel in 1948.

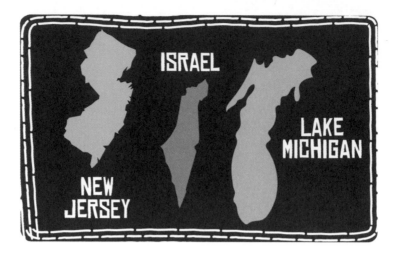

After the broad overview in chapter 36, things get even more interesting. In chapter 37, we zoom into the period leading up to the rebirth of Israel. Ezekiel's prophecy about the valley of dry bones is specifically about the rebirth of the nation of Israel at a time when her people were all but dead. In my opinion, it is no coincidence that one of the most well-known and heartbreaking historical records of the Holocaust are the pictures of Jewish people in concentration camps, starved so severely that they were merely skin and bones.

As you read these select verses from chapter 37, think about the circumstances that led to the rebirth of Israel in 1948:

> He said to me: "Son of man, these bones are the people of Israel. They say, 'Our bones are dried up and our hope is gone; we are cut off.' Therefore prophesy and say to them: 'This is what the Sovereign Lord says: My people, I am going to open your graves and bring you up from them; I will bring you back to the land of Israel. Then you, my people, will know that I am the Lord, when I open your graves and bring you up from them. I will put my Spirit in you and you will live, and I will settle you in your own land. Then you will know that I the Lord have spoken, and I have done it, declares the Lord'" (verses 11-14).

Then we have the additional detail that when the Jewish people came back to their homeland in the end times, they would unite in a single country. If you'll recall, after King Solomon's death, Israel and Judah had split into two countries due to a civil war. Here in Ezekiel 37:17, we read, "Join them together into one stick so that they will become one in your hand."

So, to recap, Ezekiel 36–37 details a time when the people of Israel would be scattered all over the world and as good as dead. Their land would lie desolate during their dispersion. Then God would bring them back from the brink and lead them into their own land once again.

And what happens next?

Chapters 38–39 go on to describe a future attack on Israel led by modern-day Russia, Turkey, and Iran (with some other allies in the mix). This invasion will come from the northern border for the specific purpose of taking valuable goods from Israel. This battle is said to occur "in that day"—in other words, in the same general time frame when Israel becomes a nation again.

Ezekiel chapters 36–37 began to be fulfilled in the late 1800s when Theodor Herzl's first Zionist Conference called for a national homeland for the Jewish people. In fulfillment of Bible prophecy, Israel miraculously became a nation again in 1948, and Jewish people from all over the world have continued streaming back to their homeland in increasingly larger numbers.

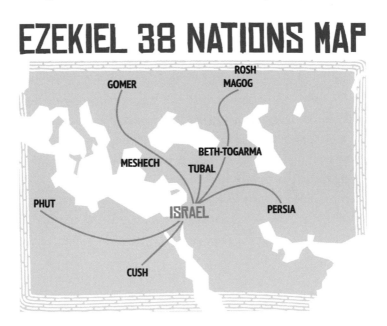

Fast-forward to our day, and Jewish people are still coming back. At the same time, we're also watching the groundwork for Ezekiel 38–39 being laid before our eyes as—for the first time ever—Russia, Turkey, and Iran have teamed up and are building the foretold coalition in war-torn Syria on the doorstep of Israel's northern border.

The final chapters of Ezekiel (40–48) contain prophecies concerning Israel during the future millennial kingdom. So the chronology of Ezekiel 36–48 is as follows: the rebirth of Israel, followed by an end-time attack on Israel, followed by the future millennial kingdom. As mentioned at the beginning of this chapter, prophecies were often given as mountain peaks that could be seen all at once but were long distances from each other. The chronology of Israel's rebirth as a nation, followed by an end-time attack from a northern coalition, followed by Israel's long-prophesied kingdom age fits the chronology and framework of end-times events as foretold in other parts of the Bible, including Daniel 9, Matthew 24–25, and the book of Revelation.

When Will Ezekiel 38 Happen?

Prophecy teachers vary on where they place the Ezekiel 38 war in relation to the rapture, but all agree it is an end-times war, as specifically stated in the text (verses 8, 14). It will take place after the land has been desolate for a long time, the people are back in the land recovering from war, in a united country with one ruler, and living securely (37:20-22; 38:7-8).

That is exactly what has happened to Israel in modern history. And now we see the exact coalition, conditions, and chronology forming before our eyes. These prophecies could not come to pass more clearly than they are right now, except for the moment when this future attack begins and God supernaturally intervenes. It is as if someone were reading Ezekiel 38 like a movie script and directing the global players how to act!

My personal belief is that this war will take place soon after the rapture (as an opportune power/resource grab during the chaotic aftermath). Or it could happen very early in the tribulation period—perhaps as part of the second-seal judgment of war.

What Plunder?

While Israel is a supremely successful agricultural, technological, and business start-up country, for decades it has relied entirely on imported energy sources. Jewish rabbis have often joked that God blessed them with milk and honey but accidentally gave all the oil to the Arab countries.

However, in 2009, a natural gas field large enough to fill 40 percent of Israel's energy needs was discovered. The Tamar field, 15 miles off the coast of Israel, was the first of several such fields Israel would discover in 2012 and 2013. Then in 2015, a massive oil reserve ten times larger than average oil fields in other parts of the world was discovered in the Golan Heights.

What all that means is this: Prior to 2009, Israel had to import energy. But since 2019, she has become a major exporter of energy. All of this amidst reports that oil production in the surrounding countries will peak in a few short years, and the fact that Israeli energy exports to Europe will cut directly into Russia's oil sales, which are its main source of national (that is, military) funding.

With that in mind, read this telling verse found in Ezekiel 38:13: "Sheba and Dedan and the merchants of Tarshish and all her villages will say to you, 'Have you come to plunder?'" Sheba and Dedan are modern-day Saudi Arabia and the Gulf States, and many prophecy experts believe Tarshish is modern-day England. If that is the case, Tarshish's villages—other translations render this as "coastlands"—could be seen as America and other countries originally colonized by England or Spain.

In other words, Saudi Arabia, England, and America (perhaps along with some other countries) will merely protest the invasion, and this verse gives us insight into the fact that Russia will be after something valuable that Israel has. Could it be Israel's oil and gas? Prophecy experts differ on what will keep America from intervening in the conflict. My view is that America will have been crippled by the rapture (and related events) and unable to come to Israel's aid. Ahead of that, however, we are already witnessing a significant weakening of America, along with a rising antisemitism toward Israel.

Perhaps Israel's energy wealth will be one of the main reasons for the "hooks in your jaws" mentioned in Ezekiel 38:4, which will "turn...around" the leader of Russia from his country's affairs and draw him into a war.

THE AMAZINGLY ACCURATE FULFILLMENTS OF PROPHECY

The strange and epic prophecies in the book of Ezekiel are fascinating to study. You'll find that it's worth the time to pick one or two prophecies from the book and study them in depth. In doing so, your faith will be strengthened as you see the amazing accuracy with which God fulfills prophecy—and you will be greatly encouraged as you see the stage being so clearly set in our day for key end-times prophecies that are relatively soon to be fulfilled. The study of prophecy enriches our appreciation for God's Word and helps us to recognize it as a supernatural handbook that prepares us for the incredible days in which we live!

CHAPTER 9

The Panoramic Prophecies of Daniel

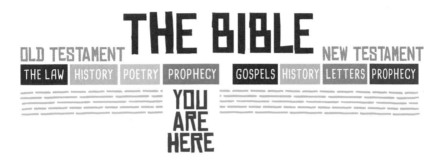

THE BIBLE

OLD TESTAMENT | NEW TESTAMENT

THE LAW | HISTORY | POETRY | PROPHECY | GOSPELS | HISTORY | LETTERS | PROPHECY

YOU ARE HERE

Seventy "sevens" are decreed for your people and your holy city to finish transgression, to put an end to sin, to atone for wickedness, to bring in everlasting righteousness, to seal up vision and prophecy and to anoint the Most Holy Place.

—DANIEL 9:24

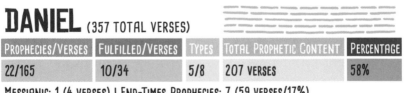

DANIEL (357 TOTAL VERSES)

PROPHECIES/VERSES	FULFILLED/VERSES	TYPES	TOTAL PROPHETIC CONTENT	PERCENTAGE
22/165	10/34	5/8	207 VERSES	58%

MESSIANIC: 1 (4 VERSES) | END-TIMES PROPHECIES: 7 (59 VERSES/17%)

I f you have read the previous chapters, you'll be familiar with the concept of the mountain peaks of Bible prophecy. This refers to prophetic events that have both near and distant fulfillments appearing in the same passage or even the same verse. You can see the peaks simultaneously, but the valleys in between, which you can't see, may stretch for hundreds of years between the peaks. In the book of Daniel, we find mountain peaks of prophecy as well, but we also find more sweeping panoramic prophecies too.

Daniel recorded some prophecies that began contemporaneously then unfold in a series of progressive and chronological events all the way into the end times. Daniel chapters 2, 7, and 9 in particular contain some of the most all-encompassing prophecies of the entire Bible. Apart from the details that concern yet-future end-times events, these prophecies span thousands of years and include scores of details that have been accurately fulfilled to the very letter.

Most of us are familiar with the narrative sections of Daniel—the lions' den, the fiery furnace, the handwriting on the wall, etc. These historical sections are filled with relevant applications for us today, giving us insight and encouragement on how to live for the Lord faithfully in an increasingly pagan culture.

Surrounding those wonderful narrative sections of Daniel are many prophetic passages. Of the 12 chapters in Daniel, eight of them are prophetic in nature—a full two-thirds of the book. Written around 537 BC, the book of Daniel accurately details the four successive kingdoms from the Babylonian Empire to the Roman Empire, along with a clear description of Western Europe during the end times. Daniel chapter 9 (especially the last four verses) surveys Israel's entire prophetic history from Daniel's time through the future tribulation period and millennial kingdom.

In addition to those sweeping overviews, Daniel also predicted key details about the conquests of Alexander the Great and the collapse and division of the Greek Empire. Furthermore, the prophet accurately predicted key events related to the intertestamental period (the time between the Old and New Testaments)—particularly historical details about the Seleucids and the actions of the evil ruler Antiochus Epiphanies (a prototype of the future end-times ruler commonly referred to as the antichrist).

As we study Daniel, it's important to recognize that certain sections of the book are not in chronological order. Instead, the book is organized into sections that relate to Israel and sections that relate to the Gentile nations. Interestingly, chapter 1 was written in Hebrew, chapters 2–7 were written in Aramaic (the Gentile language of the day), and chapters 8–12 switch back to Hebrew. The language used in each section is directly related to the people group impacted by the prophecies contained in those chapters.

Here is an outline of the book of Daniel. Note the amount of prophetic content:

Chapter 1:	Daniel in Captivity
***Chapter 2:	Nebuchadnezzar's dream of a statue and Daniel's interpretation
Chapter 3:	Image of gold and the fiery furnace
*Chapter 4:	Nebuchadnezzar's dream of the tree and Daniel's interpretation
Chapter 5:	A new king (Belshazzar) and handwriting on the wall
Chapter 6:	Another new king (Cyrus) and Daniel in the lions' den
*Chapter 7:	Daniel has a dream of four beasts that parallels the statue vision in chapter 2
*Chapter 8:	Daniel has a vision of a ram and a goat (Greece vs. Medo-Persia)
** *Chapter 9:	Daniel is visited by an angel and receives the prophecy of the 70 "weeks"
*Chapter 10:	Daniel's vision of a mysterious messenger
** *Chapter 11:	The messenger reveals more about the future of Greece, a prototype of the antichrist, and tribulation/end-time events
**Chapter 12:	The messenger reveals more details about the future tribulation period

* contains future prophecies from Daniel's perspective
** contains end-times-specific prophecies from our perspective

THE SUCCESSION OF WORLD KINGDOMS

In Daniel chapter 2, we read of a vision and an interpretation that reveals a major 2,600-year-old prophecy that identifies a succession of world empires and the empire that will come about in the end times. This prophecy is so

DANIEL CHAPTER 2

- GOLD
- SILVER
- BRONZE
- IRON
- IRON AND CLAY

grand in scope and accurate in its description that Bible critics either have to ignore it or invent weak arguments in an attempt to explain away its accuracy or the fact Daniel wrote his book before these events happened.

The successive kingdoms of Babylon, Medo-Persia, Greece, and Rome, followed by the Roman Empire splitting into two legs (fulfilled in AD 395 when the Eastern leg separated from Rome and established its capital in Constantinople, which is modern-day Istanbul), then breaking into individual nation-states, is an accurate description of history.

Daniel then shows us that the final configuration of the area ruled by the Roman Empire in the last days—the feet and toes—will be struck by a rock that completely destroys the statue. Then, according to the vision, the rock will become a mountain and fill the whole earth (Daniel 2:34-35).

Prophecy experts take this to mean that a revived but unstable Roman Empire of sorts will be in place before or at least by the early part of the tribulation period, and that this empire will be utterly destroyed when Christ returns to set up his millennial kingdom. We are given this interpretation in Daniel 2:44-45:

> In the time of those kings, the God of heaven will set up a kingdom that will never be destroyed, nor will it be left to another people. It will crush all those kingdoms and bring them to an end, but it will itself endure forever. This is the meaning of the vision of the rock cut out of a mountain, but not by human hands—a rock that broke the iron, the bronze, the clay, the silver and the gold to pieces. The great God has shown the king what will take place in the future. The dream is true and its interpretation is trustworthy.

Through the ages, various historical figures have tried and failed to revive the Roman Empire. Most notably, Napoleon tried in the early 1800s, and later, Hitler tried to do the same with his attempted 1,000-year Third Reich.

Most prophecy experts see the current European Union as the foundation for—if not the actual—end-times configuration of the statue's feet. They see the ten toes as ten elite rulers who will rule for a short time with the antichrist. The ten horns described in Revelation 17:12 support this idea, saying that they are ten rulers.

THE PERSON OF THE ANTICHRIST

The book of Daniel provides the most complete picture of the antichrist found in the Old Testament. This evil end-time ruler is referred to as the antichrist only in the books of 1 and 2 John. In 1 John 2:18, we read, "Dear children, this is the last hour; and as you have heard that the antichrist is coming, even now many antichrists have come. This is how we know it is the last hour."

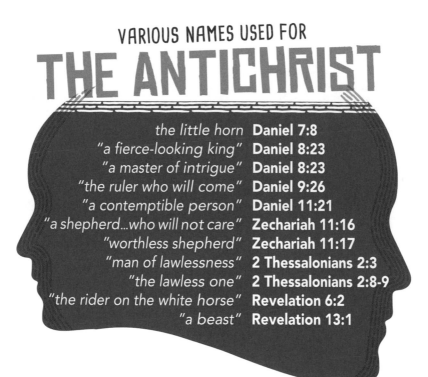

VARIOUS NAMES USED FOR

THE ANTICHRIST

the little horn	**Daniel 7:8**
"a fierce-looking king"	**Daniel 8:23**
"a master of intrigue"	**Daniel 8:23**
"the ruler who will come"	**Daniel 9:26**
"a contemptible person"	**Daniel 11:21**
"a shepherd...who will not care"	**Zechariah 11:16**
"worthless shepherd"	**Zechariah 11:17**
"man of lawlessness"	**2 Thessalonians 2:3**
"the lawless one"	**2 Thessalonians 2:8-9**
"the rider on the white horse"	**Revelation 6:2**
"a beast"	**Revelation 13:1**

There are several references to this evil end-time world ruler in the book of Daniel, beginning in chapter 7. Verse 8 refers to the antichrist as a little horn and gives us some details about his rise to power and his characteristics. When Daniel asked for the meaning of the prophecy, he was given the following information in verses 24-25:

> The ten horns are ten kings who will come from this kingdom. After them another king will arise, different from the earlier ones; he will subdue three kings. He will speak against the Most High and oppress his holy people and try to change the set times and the laws. The holy people will be delivered into his hands for a time, times and half a time.

Chapter 8 goes on to provide more details about this evil end-times ruler. Verses 23-25 report,

> In the latter part of their reign, when rebels have become completely wicked, a fierce-looking king, a master of intrigue, will arise. He will become very strong, but not by his own power. He will cause astounding devastation and will succeed in whatever he does. He will destroy those who are mighty, the holy people. He will cause deceit to prosper, and he will consider himself superior. When they feel secure, he will destroy many and take his stand against the Prince of princes. Yet he will be destroyed, but not by human power.

We also find in chapter 9 that the antichrist will come from the people who will destroy the temple after the death of the Messiah (this destruction was carried out by Rome in AD 70). He will also confirm or enforce a seven-year covenant with Israel and many, which he will break in the middle of the covenant (verse 27).

Finally, in Daniel 11:36-39, we read,

> The king will do as he pleases. He will exalt and magnify himself above every god and will say unheard-of things against the God of gods. He will be successful until the time of wrath is completed, for what has been determined must take place. He will show no regard for the gods of his ancestors or for the one desired

by women, nor will he regard any god, but will exalt himself above them all. Instead of them, he will honor a god of fortresses; a god unknown to his ancestors he will honor with gold and silver, with precious stones and costly gifts. He will attack the mightiest fortresses with the help of a foreign god and will greatly honor those who acknowledge him. He will make them rulers over many people and will distribute the land at a price.

So, the initial puzzle pieces we gather from the book of Daniel concerning the antichrist are many, and when we bring these details together, we can paint a fairly clear picture of this individual.

THE SEVENTY WEEKS

The most sweeping prophecy in Daniel is that of the 70 weeks (of years), found in chapter 9. This chapter (particularly the last four verses) is absolutely critical to understanding end-times theology. There is so much packed into those four verses that it is worth the time and effort to study them carefully. If you don't study anything else in Daniel 9, I would encourage you to spend time getting a grip on this section. Let's begin by reading Daniel 9:24-27, and I suggest that you read through the passage a few times before continuing on to the commentary below.

Seventy "sevens" are decreed for your people
and your holy city to finish transgression, to put an
end to sin, to atone for wickedness, to bring in everlasting righteousness, to seal up vision and prophecy and to anoint the Most Holy Place.
    Know and understand this: From the time the word goes out to restore and rebuild Jerusalem until the Anointed One, the ruler, comes, there will be seven "sevens," and sixty-two "sevens." It will

be rebuilt with streets and a trench, but in times of trouble. After the sixty-two "sevens," the Anointed One will be put to death and will have nothing. The people of the ruler who will come will destroy the city and the sanctuary. The end will come like a flood: War will continue until the end, and desolations have been decreed. He will confirm a covenant with many for one "seven." In the middle of the "seven" he will put an end to sacrifice and offering. And at the temple he will set up an abomination that causes desolation, until the end that is decreed is poured out on him.

At the beginning of Daniel 9, we find Daniel studying Bible prophecy. Based on prophecies in the book of Jeremiah, Daniel understood that the Jewish captivity in Babylon was to last 70 years. In response, we find Daniel fasting and praying. As he prays, Gabriel, a messenger angel, shows up and proclaims an incredibly broad prophecy that covers all of Jewish history.

The context of Daniel praying about the 70 years of captivity gives us the first hint that the 70 "sevens" is referring to "sevens of years." In other words, 70 sets of seven years. The accuracy of those years in the fulfillment of prophecy—which we will look at below—confirms this is exactly what Gabriel meant. The full time frame in view here is 490 years (using the Jewish 360-day lunar calendar that was in place at the time this prophecy was given).

The Full Scope of Jewish History

The foundational statement in this prophecy gives us the full scope of what it encompasses. Notice that the 70 "sevens" were decreed, or inexorably planned, for Daniel's people and their holy city. In other words, this prophecy is fixed, exact, and unchangeable. Daniel was Jewish, and the holy city of the Jewish people was and is Jerusalem. This prophecy is specifically for the Jewish people.

The Timing of the Messiah's Arrival Foretold

This amazing prophecy also stated the exact time frame for the arrival of Jesus's first coming. It foretold that there will be 69 sets of seven years, or 483 years on the Jewish calendar, between the call to "restore and rebuild Jerusalem" and the arrival of the "Anointed One" (verse 25).

We know from Nehemiah 2:1-8 that in 445 BC, King Artaxerxes allowed Nehemiah to go and rebuild Jerusalem (beginning with the walls around the city). Nehemiah 1 tells us this happened in the month of Nisan in the twentieth year of Artaxerxes. Long story short, we can identify this exact date based on historical and archeological records. Fast-forward 483 years, and this brings us to the spring of AD 32, the time of Jesus's triumphal entry into Jerusalem on Palm Sunday.

As I mentioned earlier, many credible prophecy experts have taken the time to calculate all the dates and study the historical references that back up the specific year identified in Nehemiah 2, and they make an extremely strong case that this prophecy of 483 Jewish years was fulfilled to the exact day!

Messiah's Death Prophesied

After the 62 "sevens," the Anointed One "will be put to death and will have nothing" (verse 26). This was clearly fulfilled at the cross, where Jesus died. He literally owned nothing and had to be buried in a borrowed tomb. All seemed lost—until the resurrection!

The Destruction of Jerusalem and the Temple in AD 70 Prophesied

The people of "the ruler who will come" will destroy the city and the sanctuary (verse 26). This is the first clear prophecy about the destruction of Jerusalem and the temple. This occurred in AD 70 at the hands of the Roman leader Titus, who would later become emperor.

The Tribulation Period Prophesied

We find another mountain-peak prophecy in Daniel 9 with a mysterious gap in between verses 26 and 27. This gap is where the church age fits in. Notice that in the sequence of the prophecy, we are told that the sanctuary—the temple—will be destroyed. Then, in the very next verse, we read that, among other things, the antichrist will defile the temple. For the antichrist to be able to do that means the temple must be rebuilt. This tells us there is a gap between the destruction of one temple and the rebuilding another during the end times, which will be defiled by the antichrist. Logic demands the gap. We also learn here that the antichrist will "confirm a covenant" for the final set of seven years of this prophecy, and that he will break the covenant at the midpoint of the seven years (verse 27).

The mysterious gap between the Messiah's being put to death and the beginning of the last set of seven years—the tribulation period—is where we are now. We are living in the gap between verses 26 and 27. During this time, God is focusing on the salvation of people in the Gentile nations. But when the antichrist confirms the seven-year covenant with Israel, the final week of Daniel's 70-weeks prophecy will begin, and the clock will resume ticking toward the end of the 490 years seen in Daniel 9:24-27.

KNOWLEDGE AND TRAVEL INCREASED

In Daniel 12:4, we gain critical insight into a key end-time sign. An angelic messenger delivers a message to Daniel that talks about end-times events, including the tribulation. Then the angel said, "But you, Daniel, roll up and seal the words of the scroll until the time of the end. Many will go here and there to increase knowledge."

In other words, the prophecies in Daniel would not make much sense to people for most of history, but as the end of the age approached, "the words of the scroll" would be unsealed. This unsealing would occur at a time when "many will go here and there to increase knowledge." This refers to great technological advances in travel and human knowledge. With that in mind, consider the following facts.

Less than 200 years ago, the fastest way to travel was on horseback. In the year 1825, the first public steam railway was introduced. Airplanes didn't come along until December 14, 1903, when Wilbur Wright successfully flew for a whopping three seconds. Since then, we've broken the sound barrier, been to the moon and back, set up an international space station, and made worldwide travel easily accessible to just about everyone.

Until the early 1900s, human knowledge doubled about every century. By the end of World War II, knowledge doubled every 25 years.[3] Today there are so many forms of new knowledge that we can't keep up.

In addition to general human knowledge, many prophecy experts point out that these verses may also indicate that end-times prophecies will be *unlocked* in the last days. This means that many prophetic passages that have not been understood in the past are becoming clear to our generation, resulting in greatly increased prophetic knowledge as we study the Scriptures and consider current events.

A GRAND VIEW OF PROPHETIC HISTORY

If I had to use only one book of the Bible to convince a skeptic to study in light of its accurate predictions about history, it would be the book of Daniel. Critics of the Bible have long known about the incredible accuracy of the prophecies in the book—so much so that they used to argue that Daniel had to be written after the fact. But, as mentioned previously, the discovery of the Dead Sea Scrolls proved that the book of Daniel was already a well-established ancient text by 200 BC. That caused a major problem for critics who claimed Daniel was written after the fact because many of the prophecies in the book were fulfilled well after 200 BC.

When Daniel was given the end-times prophecies that are detailed in the book, sometimes he felt disturbed, and other times he wanted to know more. In Daniel 12:8-10, we read,

> I heard, but I did not understand. So I asked, "My lord, what will the outcome of all this be?" He replied, "Go your way, Daniel, because the words are

rolled up and sealed until the time of the end. Many will be purified, made spotless and refined, but the wicked will continue to be wicked. None of the wicked will understand, but those who are wise will understand."

Jesus even informed his disciples in Matthew 13:17 that "many prophets and righteous people longed to see what you see but did not see it, and to hear what you hear but did not hear it." The prophets yearned to see the arrival of the Messiah and the restoration of all things. We are privileged to be able to see—in hindsight—the fulfillment of prophecies related to the first coming of the Messiah. We're also the first generation in almost 2,000 years that has witnessed the fulfillment of prophecy with the rebirth of Israel, the continual growth (in terms of population, financial strength, and military might) of the nation, and key stage-setting events that are preparing future prophecies to be fulfilled.

The panoramic prophecies of Daniel are extremely compelling, faith-building, and exciting for any student of prophecy who takes the time and effort to explore them.

CHAPTER 10

The Not-So-Minor Prophets

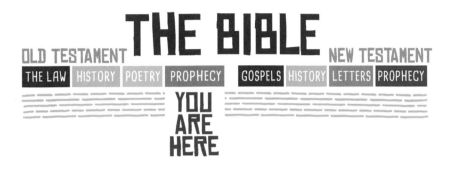

THE BIBLE

OLD TESTAMENT | NEW TESTAMENT

THE LAW | HISTORY | POETRY | PROPHECY | GOSPELS | HISTORY | LETTERS | PROPHECY

YOU ARE HERE

In the last days the mountain of the LORD's temple will be established as the highest of the mountains; it will be exalted above the hills, and peoples will stream to it.

—MICAH 4:1

One milestone a dad both cherishes and dreads is the moment when his child beats him at some physical feat or competition. I have always been a fast sprinter and could always outdo my kids in a footrace—until one fateful day. I distinctly remember when my oldest son, Daniel, beat me in a sprint for the first time. It happened after one of his soccer practices, when he was 15 or 16 years old. He had been playing high-level club soccer for years, and one day after practice, someone kicked a ball past us and we both took off running to see who could get to it

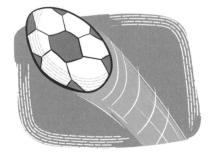

first. Even though Daniel had already gone through 1.5 hours of intense practice and conditioning, he still beat me by a few steps!

Fast-forward a couple of years, and I was in a similar spur-of-the-moment competition with my daughter, Natalie, who is 17 months younger than Daniel. She is shorter in stature than most of her fellow soccer players, but growing up with two brothers had made her surprisingly powerful and aggressive—beyond what you would have expected when you first witnessed her stepping onto the field.

In our friendly competition, Natalie and I both raced to a ball that was kicked about 60 feet beyond where we were standing. For the record, my daughter did not beat me. I had her by a step, but little did I know she had something else up her sleeve. Even though I weigh over 200 pounds, during a full sprint, my 5'2" and 120-pound daughter skillfully planted her opposite foot at the opportune moment, lowered her shoulder, and knocked me four feet away from the ball!

She had learned to use her God-given skill set and training to her advantage against a much bigger and still slightly faster male opponent!

I was really surprised by Natalie's strength and agility. I had seen it on the field, but that was the first time I had experienced it for myself. Her power-packed signature move had knocked many opponents off the soccer ball, and I became her latest victim! Both events—when my son beat me to the ball, and when my daughter knocked me off the ball—are etched in my memory as proud moments when I witnessed my children excel at something and beat their old man.

Like my daughter, the minor prophets pack a punch that is more significant than you might expect. These books are referred to as minor simply because of their shorter lengths. As part of Scripture, they're just as significant as the major prophets. Unfortunately, many readers have neglected these books because of their seeming lack of relevance to the rest of the Bible or to our daily lives.

I believe that one reason people have a hard time understanding the book of Revelation or the order of events during the end times (called the Day of the Lord by the Old Testament prophets) is because they have never read the books of the prophets—including the minor prophets! These shorter versions of their major counterparts are densely packed with riveting information related to the first and second advents of the Messiah. They also help students to understand the chronology of the Old Testament and what led up to the New Testament period.

Below I've included the statistics related to the amount of prophecy in each book along with some key prophetic features and themes that stood out to me as I researched and studied these amazing, power-packed books.

HOSEA

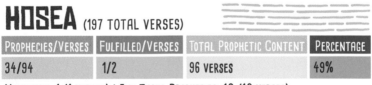

HOSEA (197 TOTAL VERSES)

PROPHECIES/VERSES	FULFILLED/VERSES	TOTAL PROPHETIC CONTENT	PERCENTAGE
34/94	1/2	96 VERSES	49%

MESSIANIC: 1 (1 VERSES) | END-TIMES PROPHECIES: 10 (10 VERSES)

Hosea was a prophet to the northern kingdom of Israel at the same time Isaiah and Micah were ministering to the southern kingdom of Judah. Hosea's wife, Gomer, was unfaithful and served as an object lesson of Israel's unfaithfulness to the Lord. The first three chapters of Hosea detail this aspect of his domestic life, and the remainder of the book presents key messages from Hosea's 50-year ministry as a prophet. Similar to the other prophetic books in the Old Testament, his key messages highlight the sins and unfaithfulness of the people, the coming judgment, and the all-important fact of God's continued love for his people.

There are a few interesting passages to note from the book of Hosea.

Resurrection and Revival

I consulted some reliable commentaries to do research on Hosea 6:2, which says, "After two days will he revive us; on the third day he will restore us, that we may live in his presence." The commentators observed that the passage is either a reference to the resurrection of Christ (being raised on the third day), or to the reviving of the Jewish people at the end of the tribulation period, when they call on the Lord once again. The entire chapter is worth reading and is heavily prophetic, with details about the Lord coming to the Jewish people.

Wanderers Among the Nations

Hosea also includes prophecies that clearly predicted the Jewish people would be scattered around the world, then they would eventually be healed and reconciled with their God. Note these two verses from Hosea chapters 9 and 14:

Wanderers

> My God will reject them because they have not obeyed him; they will be wanderers among the nations (9:17).

Reconciliation

> I will heal their waywardness and love them freely, for my anger has turned away from them (14:4).

JOEL

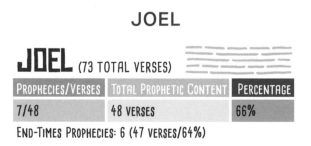

JOEL (73 TOTAL VERSES)		
PROPHECIES/VERSES	TOTAL PROPHETIC CONTENT	PERCENTAGE
7/48	48 VERSES	66%

END-TIMES PROPHECIES: 6 (47 VERSES/64%)

Joel and his book are a bit more mysterious than the other minor prophets. A clear time frame for the book is elusive to pin down—perhaps providentially so. The book is a response to a severe drought and series of locust invasions that took place sometime during Israel's ancient history.

As I mentioned a few chapters ago in my introduction to the book of Isaiah, the Day of the Lord can refer to any time that God intervenes in history to judge a nation, but the phrase is most often used in an end-times sense. Joel used what he saw as God's punishment as an occasion to point to a future time of global judgment known as the Day of the Lord—a major theme in the book of Joel. If there were one book of the Old Testament that is best known for its focus on the Day of the Lord, it is the book of Joel!

It's helpful to have an outline of the book to figure out when Joel is speaking of the events of his day versus the prophesied events of the future tribulation period.

1. Plague of locusts (1:1-14)
2. Pointing to the eschatological Day of the Lord (prelude) (1:15–2:32)
3. Additional details about the Day of the Lord (3)

Here are a couple other key passages to consider:

Joel 2:32

> Everyone who calls on the name of the LORD will be saved; for on Mount Zion and in Jerusalem there will be deliverance, as the LORD has said, even among the survivors whom the LORD calls.

This verse further supports the truth that one day an entire remnant of Jewish people will realize that Jesus was indeed the Messiah (Zechariah 12:20; Matthew 23:39; Romans 11:26).

Joel 3:1-2

> In those days and at that time, when I restore the fortunes of Judah and Jerusalem, I will gather all nations and bring them down to the Valley of Jehoshaphat. There I will put them on trial for what they did to my inheritance, my people Israel, because they scattered my people among the nations and divided up my land.

Notice that Joel seems to indicate that the great end-times battle (he seems to be speaking of the Armageddon campaign) will take place in the same general period of history as Israel's restoration.

Then we find a clear division between the now-familiar chronology of the tribulation period followed by the future kingdom age:

Joel 3:9-16: Tribulation period (compare with Revelation 19:11-21)

Joel 3:17-21: Millennial kingdom (compare with Revelation 20:1-6)

AMOS

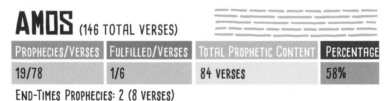

AMOS (146 TOTAL VERSES)

PROPHECIES/VERSES	FULFILLED/VERSES	TOTAL PROPHETIC CONTENT	PERCENTAGE
19/78	1/6	84 VERSES	58%

END-TIMES PROPHECIES: 2 (8 VERSES)

The book of Amos follows a similar pattern and presents the same themes as several of the other prophets: a call to repentance or immediate judgment will come, followed by promises of God's unfailing love and future blessing, along with distant-fulfillment prophecies about the end times.

The theme of Israel's restoration is key in the book of Amos. Notice the progression of restoration followed by the kingdom age when you consider Amos 9:11-15.

> "In that day I will restore David's fallen shelter—I will repair its broken walls and restore its ruins—and will rebuild it as it used to be, so that they may possess the remnant of Edom and all the nations

that bear my name," declares the LORD, who will do these things. "The days are coming," declares the LORD, "when the reaper will be overtaken by the plowman and the planter by the one treading grapes. New wine will drip from the mountains and flow from all the hills, and I will bring my people Israel back from exile. They will rebuild the ruined cities and live in them. They will plant vineyards and drink their wine; they will make gardens and eat their fruit. I will plant Israel in their own land, never again to be uprooted from the land I have given them," says the LORD your God.

OBADIAH

OBADIAH (21 TOTAL VERSES)

PROPHECIES/VERSES	PERCENTAGE
3/8	38%

END-TIMES PROPHECIES: 1 (7 VERSES)

As with other books of the prophets, we see the near and far mountain peaks of prophecy present in Obadiah. We also continue to see the 100 percent accuracy of the fulfillment of Bible prophecy. Obadiah 18 says, "'There will be no survivors from Esau.' The LORD has spoken." Today, there are no survivors of the once-mighty Edomites. In contrast, the Israelites are thriving and continuing to regather in their homeland today.

Obadiah is a single-chapter book yet is highly prophetic. The first half (verses 1-14) contains prophecy with near fulfillment events, and, as usual, the section concerning far/end-time events (verses 15-21) follows the now-familiar chronology of the tribulation period (15-18), then the kingdom age (19-21).

JONAH

JONAH (48 TOTAL VERSES)

PROPHECIES/VERSES	TYPES	TOTAL PROPHETIC CONTENT	PERCENTAGE
2/2	1/1	3 VERSES	6%

Some have suggested that the book of Jonah is merely an allegory, but there is no biblical reason to hold that view. In 2 Kings 14:25, he is cited as a real prophet from Gath Hepher (near Nazareth, interestingly enough). Jesus spoke of Jonah as a literal person who was literally swallowed by a fish (Matthew 12:39-41). In terms of extrabiblical evidence, we do find that around 810–783 BC (during the reign of Adad-nirari III), the people of Assyria exhibited a leaning toward monotheism. It's also possible that the citywide repentance in Nineveh occurred around 771–754 BC (during the reign of Ashduran III), following the plague of 765 BC, the eclipse in 763 BC, and another plague in 759 BC. If Jonah's message was delivered after those three attention-getting events, it would make sense for the population-wide repentance to have occurred.

As far as I can tell, the only key prophetic detail in Jonah is his three days in the belly of the fish. Jesus used this in Matthew 12:39 to point to his death, burial, and resurrection when he said, "A wicked and adulterous generation asks for a sign! But none will be given it except the sign of the prophet Jonah."

MICAH

MICAH (105 TOTAL VERSES)

PROPHECIES/VERSES	PERCENTAGE
11/55	52%

END-TIMES PROPHECIES: 3 (19 VERSES/18%)

Micah warned of coming judgment, highlighted the reasons it was coming, and specified how it would come to the leaders and the false prophets. Then in chapter 4, Micah switched gears and told of a coming kingdom "in the last days" (4:1).

Micah then hopped back and forth on the mountain peaks of prophecy. In the second half of chapter 4, he spoke of the immediate/impending judgment of his day. Then in chapter 5, he "stood" on later mountain peaks as he prophesied events of the first coming (verses 2-3) and the second coming (verses 4-15). Chapter 6 and most of chapter 7 recount God's indictment of Israel and her personified replies. Finally, in 7:11-20, Micah recalled and proclaimed God's unfailing love and future blessing of Israel.

NAHUM

Roughly 100 years had passed since the people of Nineveh had repented in response to Jonah's warning of judgment. Apparently, the generation that had

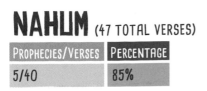

NAHUM (47 TOTAL VERSES)

PROPHECIES/VERSES	PERCENTAGE
5/40	85%

repented was not successful in passing their beliefs on to the next generation, which quickly descended into the evil, cruel, and pagan ways of their pre-repentance ancestors. Nahum prophesied against Nineveh and, in a short three chapters, warned the people of the judgment that was soon to come. Indeed, the once-powerful and feared Ninevites experienced God's wrath and were wiped out.

HABAKKUK

HABAKKUK (56 TOTAL VERSES)

PROPHECIES/VERSES	PERCENTAGE
5/16	29%

END-TIMES PROPHECIES: 1 (14 VERSES)

Habakkuk is different than the other prophets' books in this way: Most of the prophets talked to people for God, but Habakkuk questioned God and God talked back to Habakkuk.

The short book begins with Habakkuk's problems and ends with his praises to God. The book is a defense of God's goodness even though evil is allowed—for a season.

In Habakkuk 2:3, we read this compelling promise: "The revelation awaits an appointed time; it speaks of the end and will not prove false. Though it linger, wait for it; it will certainly come and will not delay."

In the New Testament, God repeats this sentiment in 2 Peter 3:9, where we read, "The Lord is not slow in keeping his promise, as some understand slowness. Instead he is patient with you, not wanting anyone to perish, but everyone to come to repentance."

In other words, you can bank on the fact that Bible prophecy will be fulfilled exactly as foretold. There is no such thing as delayed prophetic fulfillment. Everything happens exactly according to God's plan. We can rest in His sovereignty, perfect timing, and impeccable promise-keeping.

In Habakkuk 2:14, we read this beautifully poetic description of the future millennial kingdom: "The earth will be filled with the knowledge of the glory of the LORD as the waters cover the sea."

ZEPHANIAH

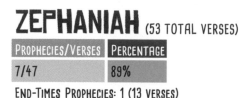

ZEPHANIAH (53 TOTAL VERSES)

PROPHECIES/VERSES	PERCENTAGE
7/47	89%

END-TIMES PROPHECIES: 1 (13 VERSES)

Zephaniah shared both near and distant prophecies of judgment for the immediate time frame as well as the future Day of the Lord. In a familiar prophetic pattern, Zephaniah ended his book on a high note with a glorious description of the blessings Gentiles and Jews will experience in the millennial kingdom, which—as we've discussed previously—is often seen as part of the Day of the Lord.

The prophetic sequence of the tribulation followed by the kingdom age is echoed here in Zephaniah, with the tribulation period described in 1:14-19; 3:8; and the millennial kingdom in 3:9-20.

HAGGAI

HAGGAI (38 TOTAL VERSES)

PROPHECIES/VERSES	PERCENTAGE
3/8	21%

END-TIMES PROPHECIES: 3 (4 VERSES)

Haggai's short two-chapter book contains four calls—each beginning with the phrase, "This is what the Lord Almighty says." The four calls are to build the temple, to be courageous, to live righteously, and to look forward to God's future blessing.

Haggai 2:6-9 also echoes the familiar order of events that places the tribulation period first, and the kingdom age afterward:

> This is what the Lord Almighty says: "In a little while I will once more shake the heavens and the earth, the sea and the dry land. I will shake all nations, and what is desired by all nations will come, and I will fill this house with glory," says the Lord Almighty. "The silver is mine and the gold is mine," declares the Lord Almighty. "The glory of this present house will be greater than the glory of the former house," says the Lord Almighty. "And in this place I will grant peace," declares the Lord Almighty.

ZECHARIAH (211 TOTAL VERSES)

PROPHECIES/VERSES	PERCENTAGE
17/134	64%

MESSIANIC: 1 (8 VERSES) | END-TIMES PROPHECIES: 6 (36 VERSES/17%)

Much of the symbolism found in Zechariah's visions alludes to the book of Revelation. Zechariah chapter 12 contains a key messianic prophecy that highlights the critical link between the first and second advents. In verse 10, we read, "They will look on me, the one they have pierced, and they will mourn for him as one mourns for an only child, and grieve bitterly for him as one grieves for a firstborn son." The chronological context of this verse is the end times, and the ethnic context is Jewish. At the return of Christ at the end of the tribulation, the Jewish "hardening in part" spoken of in Romans 11:25 will be lifted and the people will realize that Jesus was their Messiah all along! It is at this point when "all Israel will be saved" (verse 26).

The final chapter of the book provides key details about the tribulation period. Here, we learn that at Christ's return (either before or after he destroys the armies of the antichrist), he will set his feet down upon the Mount of Olives and it will split in two. This is the same place where he gave his famous end-time teaching known as the Olivet Discourse (Matthew 24–25; Mark 13; Luke 21). It is also the same place where Jesus ascended into heaven (Luke 24:50-51).

Zechariah 12 says Israel will be like a "firepot in a woodpile" in the last days. Even though this country is tiny and makes every effort to be at peace with her Arab neighbors, hundreds of rockets can be fired into her civilian neighborhoods without any real condemnation from the UN, EU, or many countries around the world, with the general exception of the US. Yet God says this about Israel:

> I am going to make Jerusalem a cup that sends all the surrounding peoples reeling. Judah will be besieged as well as Jerusalem. On that day, when all the nations of the earth are gathered against her, I will make Jerusalem an immovable rock for all the nations. All who try to move it will injure themselves (verses 2-3).

MALACHI (55 TOTAL VERSES)

PROPHECIES/VERSES	PERCENTAGE
10/22	40%

MESSIANIC: 1 (1 VERSE) | END-TIMES PROPHECIES: 2 (9 VERSES)

Like many of the other prophets, Malachi ended his book with prophecies about the future Day of the Lord. Interestingly, the final word of the Old Testament is "curse" (4:6 NKJV). Thus began 400 years of silence from the Lord. After this, a lot of interesting history took place, but there were no more prophetic voices until we get to the New Testament.

Malachi 4:1-6 talks about the tribulation period (also known as the Day of the Lord, or Daniel's seventieth week) followed by the Lord's return and Israel's victory:

> "Surely the day is coming; it will burn like a furnace. All the arrogant and every evildoer will be stubble, and the day that is coming will set them on fire," says the LORD Almighty. "Not a root or a branch will be left to them. But for you who revere my name, the sun of righteousness will rise with healing in its rays. And you will go out and frolic like well-fed calves. Then you will trample on the wicked; they will be ashes under the soles of your feet on the day when I act," says the LORD Almighty. Remember the law of my servant Moses, the decrees and laws I gave him at Horeb for all Israel. See, I will send the prophet Elijah to you before that great and dreadful day of the LORD comes. He will turn the hearts of the parents to their children, and the hearts of the children to their parents; or else I will come and strike the land with total destruction."

As we'll see in the next chapter, John the Baptist came in the spirit of Elijah. In a sense, everything could have been fulfilled at the first coming of Christ, but because the Jewish people and leadership rejected him at that time, everything prophesied (dispersion and mistreatment of the Jewish people) took place, and in the end times (after the rapture, I believe), Elijah will literally enter the scene before the tribulation period begins. More on that in the next chapter and in chapter 14. How's that for a cliffhanger?

SETTING THE STAGE FOR THE NEW TESTAMENT

As you can see, the minor prophets are anything but minor. If anything, their brevity allows careful students of Bible prophecy to carefully process and study the amazing prophetic details included in these heavily eschatological records from the time of the prophets. Included in this section of Scripture are many key pieces to the end-times puzzle that help provide clarity for other key sections, such as the Olivet Discourse (Jesus's teaching on the end times) and the all-important final book of the Bible, Revelation.

With the end of the Old Testament came 400 years of prophetic silence as God worked in history to fulfill prophecy and prepare the way for the coming of the Messiah Jesus, who arrived on the scene at just the right time (Galatians 4:4-5). Prophetic silence did not mean divine inactivity. On the contrary, God was busy fulfilling prophecy and setting the stage for act two of the grand narrative.

CHAPTER 11

Prophecy Meets History
(The Gospels and Acts)

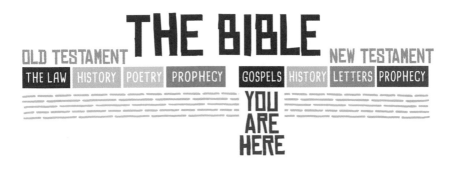

THE BIBLE

OLD TESTAMENT				NEW TESTAMENT			
THE LAW	HISTORY	POETRY	PROPHECY	GOSPELS	HISTORY	LETTERS	PROPHECY

YOU
ARE
HERE

He has set a day when he will judge the world with justice
by the man he has appointed. He has given proof of
this to everyone by raising him from the dead.

—ACTS 17:31

Have you ever heard of a shock-wave vortex? If you pause to think about it, you'll realize that phrase is an oxymoron. Shock waves reverberate outward from the point of an explosion. A vortex draws things inward to a central point of compression. Well after the long buildup of the first 39 books of the Bible and the first 4,000 or so years of earth's history, the events of the Gospels and the birth of the church explode on the scene with shock waves that echo into eternity past and eternity future. While at the same time, all historically prophetic events related to the first advent converge into the vortex of the death and resurrection of the Messiah.

The sacrificial death of Christ and his victorious resurrection over sin and death combine to give us the single most impactful set of events the world has ever seen. And they were long prophesied in Scripture by a God who is outside of time and tells history in advance.

The four Gospels (written AD 40–95), which provide four accounts of Jesus's life and ministry, and the book of Acts (written AD 60–61), which traces the spread of the gospel around the known world, set the stage for the remaining bits of revealed theological truth found in the letters of the New Testament. Let's take a look now at the prophetic significance of the Gospels and the book of Acts to see how prophecy played out in history in the events surrounding the first advent of the Messiah.

MATTHEW

MATTHEW (1,071 TOTAL VERSES)

PROPHECIES/VERSES	FULFILLED/VERSES	TOTAL PROPHETIC CONTENT	PERCENTAGE
58/261	32/106	367 VERSES	34%

END-TIMES PROPHECIES: 16 (138 VERSES/13%)

The two advents have always been part of God's sovereign plan, yet in one sense, the kingdom technically could have been established during Jesus's first advent had he not been rejected by the Jewish leadership and population at large (23:37-39). Matthew said that their rejection of Christ would lead to a judgment of the nation once again (23:38; 24:1-2; see also Luke 19:43-44).

Matthew's Gospel contains roughly 130 references to the Old Testament. Matthew also includes Jesus's legal ancestry (through his earthly/adopted father, Joseph) to show his Jewish lineage—that he descended from both Abraham and King David (critical details in relation to affirming his identity as the Messiah and King). Matthew also records for us 45 parables, at least 24 miracles, and the longest discourses (continuous teachings) of the Gospels.

There were more than 300 prophecies (at least 109 of them being unique or distinct) about Jesus that were fulfilled at Jesus's first advent. In the early 1950s, a famous mathematician by the name of Peter Stoner wrote a book entitled *Science Speaks*. In this book, he calculated that for one person to fulfill just eight of the 300-plus prophecies about Jesus's first coming would be as unlikely as the following scenario which I have paraphrased in my own words:

Mark a single coin (a silver dollar) with an X; fill the state of Texas two feet deep with silver dollars; mix the single marked coin in randomly anywhere in the state; blindfold a man and let him wander the state as long as he wants; finally, give the blindfolded man one chance to reach down and pick up a coin. If that coin turns out the be the marked one, that would be the same statistical probability of one man fulfilling just eight of the prophecies about the Messiah. And Jesus fulfilled more than 300! In other words, it is impossible for one man to have fulfilled the 300-plus messianic prophecies by chance.

In terms of prophetic content, we find many fulfilled prophecies that converge in the Gospels with the birth, life, ministry, death, burial, and resurrection of Jesus. Matthew contains many details of fulfilled prophecy—and in many cases directly quotes the Old Testament to highlight this fact. I discovered 15 direct quotes of Old Testament prophecies in Matthew's Gospel. These clear and purposeful connections to the Old Testament were included to prove to a Jewish audience that Jesus was indeed the long-awaited Messiah.

15 Direct Quotes in Matthew That Are from the Old Testament

1:22-23 | Isaiah 7:14 (virgin birth)

2:5-6 | Micah 5:2 (born in Bethlehem)

2:14-15 | Hosea 11:1 (called out of Egypt)

2:16-18 | Jeremiah 31:15 (murder of the innocent children)

4:13-16 | Isaiah 9:1-2 (lived in area of Zebulun and Naphtali)

8:16-17 | Isaiah 53:4 (healing the sick)

10:34-36 | Micah 7:6 (his truth will cause division)

11:9-10 | Malachi 3:1 (John the Baptist)

12:18-21 | Isaiah 42:1-4 (obscure start to ministry)

13:14-15 | Isaiah 6:9-10 (spiritually blind will miss the truth)

13:34-35 | Psalm 78:2 (speak in parables)

15:6-9 | Isaiah 29:13; Malachi 2:2 (man-made rules of religious leaders)

21:4-7 | Zechariah 9:9; see also Isaiah 62:11 (enter Jerusalem on a donkey)

21:15-16 | Psalm 8:2 (triumphal entry)

27:3-10 | Jeremiah 32:6-9; Zechariah 11:12-13 (betrayed for 30 pieces of silver)

In addition to documenting fulfilled prophecies, the book of Matthew records prophecies related to future events—from Matthew's perspective and ours as well.

Church-Age Prophecies

In Matthew 13, Jesus gives seven prophetic parables about the church age. These parables are the parable of the sower, the parable of the wheat and tares, the parable of the mustard seed, the parable of the yeast, the parable of the hidden treasure, the parable of the pearl, and the parable of the net.

All the parables have to do with the church age—which was yet future at the time Jesus taught them—and provide key prophetic details about the church age and the millennial kingdom. Two of the parables (the parable of the sower and the parable of the wheat and tares) are explained by Jesus in chapter 13.

In Matthew 13:37-43 Jesus said,

> The one who sowed the good seed is the Son of Man. The field is the world, and the good seed stands for the people of the kingdom. The weeds are the people of the evil one, and the enemy who sows

them is the devil. The harvest is the end of the age, and the harvesters are angels. As the weeds are pulled up and burned in the fire, so it will be at the end of the age. The Son of Man will send out his angels, and they will weed out of his kingdom everything that causes sin and all who do evil. They will throw them into the blazing furnace, where there will be weeping and gnashing of teeth. Then the righteous will shine like the sun in the kingdom of their Father. Whoever has ears, let them hear.

If we take the time to read through the details of those seven verses, we discover many prophetic details about the church era and the end of the age.

Olivet Discourse

The second-longest recorded teaching of Jesus is the Olivet Discourse—a prophetic look into the future that spans from the first century to the end of the future tribulation period. This message is found in Matthew 24–25, Mark 13, and Luke 21:5-36. No single passage contains every word of Jesus's teaching in the discourse, and each writer focused on different details with their particular audience in mind. A careful comparison of all three accounts provides a more complete view, and the account in Matthew is the longest version of the teaching.

Matthew 24 opens with a shocking statement to Jesus's disciples. In verses 1-3, we read,

> Jesus left the temple and was walking away when his disciples came up to him to call his attention to its buildings. "Do you see all these things?" he asked. "Truly I tell you, not one stone here will be left on another; every one will be thrown down." As Jesus was sitting on the Mount of Olives, the disciples came to him privately. "Tell us," they said, "when will this happen, and what will be the sign of your coming and of the end of the age?"

The disciples—having seen Jesus perform miracles, enter Jerusalem while being hailed as king, unleash a holy temple-tantrum in the temple courts, and defy the religious leaders in front of the crowds—began to sense that it was about to "get real" in terms of the coming kingdom. They knew a significant change had occurred. The lowly and humble countercultural teacher was now entering a new phase of ministry during which his kingdom authority began to be revealed. They did not understand the cross, the resurrection, or the long church age yet, but they sensed that a transition was taking place.

The importance of the timing of Jesus's instruction cannot be overstated. This teaching came right after he was rejected by his people—as represented by the Jewish religious leaders—and just before the events leading to his crucifixion.

All of what Jesus spoke of in the discourse was future prophecy. His words about every stone being torn down were fulfilled in exact detail a little more than 35 years after the prophecy was given.

Literally every single stone of the temple building was thrown down so that the Romans
could access all the gold that had melted
between the cracks when the temple had
been burned down during the attack on
Jerusalem. You can still see many of the
large stones lying at the base of the
Temple Mount today. We know the
rest of Jesus's prophecies will also
be fulfilled in exact detail.

Trusted prophecy teachers differ on various topics related to the
Olivet Discourse. As I mentioned in chapter 1, the only view that consistently interprets Scripture from a literal perspective is the futurist view. Within the futurist view camp, there are various views on the timing of certain end-times events. I discuss that in further detail in chapter 14. But even within the futurist, pretribulational view, scholars debate on whether Jesus was speaking of events in the tribulation era exclusively or if he also mentions details related to the end of the church age as well.

For the purposes of this book, I'll just note that all futurist scholars agree that Jesus foretold both first-century events related to the destruction of Jerusalem and end-times events related to the tribulation period.

One other very important note here is that Jesus did not chide his disciples for wanting to understand the signs of the times. On two other occasions, Jesus rebuked the religious leaders and the crowds for not understanding the signs of their day. How much more would God expect us to understand the signs of the end as we see the day approaching (Hebrews 10:25)?

Sheep and Goats Judgment

In an earlier chapter, I mentioned that I would unpack what's known as the sheep and goats judgment. It's found in Matthew 25:31-46 and is written as a short parable. In verse 31, we learn that the time frame of this judgment is when Jesus returns to set up his kingdom. So, chronologically speaking, this occurs after the tribulation period and during the transition to (or in the beginning of) the millennial kingdom.

All the survivors of the tribulation will be brought before the Lord and judged based on how they treated the Jewish people (see verses 39-40, 45). The goats are the surviving unbelievers who mistreated the Jewish people (they will have gathered in an army against God and in pursuit of the Jewish people). The sheep are the believers who survive the tribulation period. The goats will be sent to hell, which was "prepared for the devil and his angels" (verse 41).

Millennial Kingdom

In previous chapters, I have highlighted the many portions of the Old Testament that contain clear and plain language about God's permanent commitment to Israel and the Jewish people and the scriptural and prophetic necessity of a literal future kingdom age during which Jesus will rule the world from Jerusalem. We continue to discover clear and plain language supporting those prophetic truths here in the New Testament.

Here's an example from Matthew 19:27-28, where we read,

> Peter answered him, "We have left everything to follow you! What then will there be for us?" Jesus said to them, "Truly I tell you, at the renewal of all things, when the Son of Man sits on his glorious throne, you who have followed me will also sit on twelve thrones, judging the twelve tribes of Israel."

Then in Matthew 26, in the context of the last supper and his instituting the practice of communion, Jesus said, "I tell you, I will not drink from this fruit of the vine from now on until that day when I drink it new with you in my Father's kingdom" (verse 29).

Over and over again in the Old and New Testaments we read clear and plain descriptions of details concerning a literal future kingdom. We learn about the duration of this kingdom age (1,000 years) in Revelation 20. Here in the first Gospel account, we find unambiguous words from Jesus himself that confirm the coming of a literal kingdom.

Great Commission

In the final two verses of the last chapter of Matthew, we read the well-known words of the great commission: "Go and make disciples of all nations, baptizing them in the name of the Father and of the Son and of the Holy Spirit, and teaching them to obey everything I have commanded you. And surely I am with you always, to the very end of the age" (verses 19-20).

The great commission was an incredible prophecy as much as it was a command. In those two verses, Jesus predicted that Christianity would spread around the entire globe (an impossibility at the time), that his teachings would impact the entire world, and that the church age would have a duration long enough for all of this to happen. Last, but not least, he foretold that the church age would have a very clear end. These are no small prophecies. The fact that Christianity has gone global and the teachings of Christ are known worldwide once again proves that God's prophetic Word comes to pass literally. We can therefore bank on the fact that this current age will have a clear and definite end. Thankfully, Jesus promised to be with us to the very end of the age.

MARK

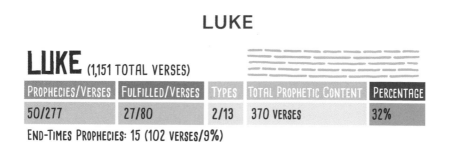

MARK (678 TOTAL VERSES)

PROPHECIES/VERSES	FULFILLED/VERSES	TYPES	TOTAL PROPHETIC CONTENT	PERCENTAGE
27/105	12/31	2/2	138 VERSES	20%

END-TIMES PROPHECIES: 17 (62 VERSES/9%)

Mark probably received most of his information from Peter and wrote his Gospel primarily to a Gentile, Roman audience. He made about 60-plus references to the Old Testament (whereas Matthew used nearly 130 and Luke used 90–100). Mark focused more on what Jesus did than on what he said, and the book is one of action and movement. The word *euthus* is used more than 40 times and is translated "at once" or "immediately." The 16-chapter book can be divided into two key sections: the service of the servant, and the sacrifice of the servant.

In Mark chapter 4, the author recorded a few of the same church-age parables that were documented in Matthew 13. Mark also includes the Olivet Discourse in chapter 13.

LUKE

LUKE (1,151 TOTAL VERSES)

PROPHECIES/VERSES	FULFILLED/VERSES	TYPES	TOTAL PROPHETIC CONTENT	PERCENTAGE
50/277	27/80	2/13	370 VERSES	32%

END-TIMES PROPHECIES: 15 (102 VERSES/9%)

Many details in the Gospel of Luke help us see that Luke was written primarily for a Gentile audience. Luke was careful to note Roman emperors and officials, and explain Jewish locations and customs. He also used the Greek translation of the Old Testament, the Septuagint, and traced Jesus's genealogy to Adam (instead of Abraham or David). As a side note, Luke cited Jesus's ancestry from Mary's genealogy, which connects back to David through his son Nathan. So, Jesus's literal bloodline (through Mary) connected him to David, and his legal ancestry through his adopted/earthly father connected him to David as well. In other words, through both Joseph and Mary, Jesus thoroughly fulfilled the prophecies about the Messiah coming from the line of David.

Like the first two Gospels, Luke recorded many details showing how key prophecies related to the first coming were fulfilled in Jesus. He also included key prophetic passages about the church age in the parable of the persistent widow (18:1-8), the parable of the ten minas (19:11-27), and the parable of the tenants (20:9-18). We also find key prophetic details about the end times in Luke 17:20-37 as well as in the Olivet Discourse in Luke 21:5-36 (also recorded by Matthew and Mark).

In addition to those key prophetic passages, here are a few more that are found in the Gospel of Luke.

In Luke chapter 1, again we see a clear distinction between first- and second-coming events, with verses 68-70 highlighting those related to the first coming, and verses 71-75 having to do with the second coming.

Luke's Playlist

We discover two songs or poetic writings in Luke 1. The first is by Mary, the mother of Jesus, and the second is by Zechariah, the father of John the Baptist. Both contain chronological details about the first and second advents of Christ.

In Luke 1:46-49, Mary speaks about events related to the first advent. In verses 50-55, she talks about the second advent. Of course, she did not realize at the time that there would be a gap between the two.

In Luke 1:68-69, Zechariah highlights details related to the first advent. In verses 71-75, he talks about the second advent. Then in the final four verses of his song (76-79), Zechariah presents the future (at the time) ministry of his son, John the Baptist.

The Foreknowledge of Jesus

Apparently, not even John the Baptist understood at the time that there would be a gap between the two advents (read Luke 3:7-9). But Jesus knew. In Luke 4, he went into the synagogue in Nazareth and read from Isaiah 61, saying, "The Spirit of the Lord is on me, because he has anointed me to proclaim good news to the poor. He has sent me to proclaim freedom for the prisoners and recovery of sight for the blind, to set the oppressed free, to proclaim the year of the Lord's favor" (verses 18-19).

Then in verses 20-21, we read, "Then he rolled up the scroll, gave it back to the attendant and sat down. The eyes of everyone in the synagogue were fastened on him. He began by saying to them, 'Today this scripture is fulfilled in your hearing.'"

What you won't realize unless you read that passage from Isaiah is that Jesus stopped mid-sentence when he rolled up the scroll. When he quoted Isaiah 61:1-2, he skipped the final phrase, "and the day of vengeance of our God, to comfort all who mourn."

Jesus told his listeners that the first part of Isaiah's prophecy (which was full of grace and proclaiming the good news to the poor, etc.) was fulfilled that very day. But he hit the pause button on the part about the day of vengeance—the future Day of the Lord, or the tribulation period.

In fact, a careful reading of the passage from Isaiah 61 reveals that it covers the first coming (verses 1-2a), the second coming (verses 2b-3a), and the future millennial kingdom (verse 3b) in chronological order—a feature that I have pointed out in other prophetic passages in the Bible.

Parable of the Persistent Widow

Most people view Luke chapter 18:1-8 as a parable that teaches the lesson, "Don't give up praying, and eventually God will answer you." But a closer examination reveals that it is a parable of the church age that gives some indication of what the time of the end will be like. The theme is that the widow was looking for justice. She had an adversary who was getting away with evil without being punished.

Verses 7-8 underscore the eschatological nature of this passage. There, we read, "Will not God bring about justice for his chosen ones, who cry out to him day and night? Will he keep putting them off? I tell you, he will see that they get justice, and quickly. However, when the Son of Man comes, will he find faith on the earth?"

This aligns with other prophecies of the end times that feature a great falling away after a long period of evil activity that seems to go unpunished. While there will be a great end-times revival on earth before the Lord returns (which we'll learn about in chapter 14 when we look at the book of Revelation), we also see a great falling away from the truth and Jesus returning to an earth where he finds, relatively speaking, few with real saving faith.

God's Sovereignty Versus Free Will

In Luke 19:41-44, we read,

> As he approached Jerusalem and saw the city, he wept over it and said, "If you, even you, had only known on this day what would bring you peace—but now it is hidden from your eyes. The days will come upon you when your enemies will build an embankment against you and encircle you and hem you in on every side. They will dash you to the ground, you and the children within your walls. They will not leave one stone on another, because you did not recognize the time of God's coming to you."

And in Matthew 10:5-7, we read, "These twelve Jesus sent out with the following instructions: 'Do not go among the Gentiles or enter any town of the Samaritans. Go rather to the lost sheep of Israel. As you go, proclaim this message: "The kingdom of heaven has come near."'"

In other words, the kingdom is here if you want it. It's up to you to accept it. Then once the Jewish people rejected it, Jesus lamented that a near judgment was about to take place (the destruction of Jerusalem in AD 70), which would later be followed by a far judgment (the destruction of the world during the tribulation), then the establishment of the kingdom.

Every key line of theology has an inherent tension between God's sovereignty and mankind's responsibility. We can't reconcile that seeming contradiction in the six inches between our ears. This tension falls into the category of the mysteries of God. He alone can both call mankind to choose to respond, and at the same time, prophesy specific future events that are to come to pass because of mankind's rejection of the Messiah.

More Evidence for a Literal Future Kingdom

In Luke 22, we have another crystal-clear and compelling prophecy from Jesus that supports the idea that the prophecies of a literal future kingdom on earth are still yet unfulfilled. At the last supper, as recorded in verses 17-18, we read, "After taking the cup, he gave thanks and said, 'Take this and divide it among you. For I tell you I will not drink again from the fruit of the vine until the kingdom of God comes.'" Then several verses later, Jesus said, "I confer on you a kingdom, just as my Father conferred one on me, so that you may eat and drink at my table in my kingdom and sit on thrones, judging the twelve tribes of Israel" (verses 29-30).

It simply does not get any clearer than that. If we take God at his word and abide by a literal, logical, face-value interpretation of the Bible, we will arrive at the conclusion that there is coming a literal, physical kingdom on earth that will be ruled by Christ.

JOHN

JOHN (879 TOTAL VERSES)

PROPHECIES/VERSES	FULFILLED/VERSES	TOTAL PROPHETIC CONTENT	PERCENTAGE
56/102	25/52	154 VERSES	18%

MESSIANIC: 2 (6 VERSES) | END-TIMES PROPHECIES: 16 (20 VERSES)

Key Focal Points

John's primary messages are that Jesus is divine and that he is the Savior of all who believe in him. In case there are any doubts that Jesus is God himself, John drives this point home clearly in his Gospel. John chooses not to include any of Jesus's parables nor his genealogy, but focuses instead on the divine nature of Christ.

The opening verses of the book establish Jesus's divinity, and this theme is carried through the 21 chapters of the book in various ways, including a series of "I am" statements (4:24, 26; 6:35; 8:12, 24, 28, 58; 10:7, 9, 11, 14; 11:25; 13:19; 14:6; 15:1, 5). "I AM" was the Old Testament name for God (Exodus 3:14).

In John's Gospel we also find additional support for God's unconditional commitment to the Jewish people and the idea that he came first to his people. In John 1:31, we read these clear words from John the Baptist: "I myself did not know him, but the reason I came baptizing with water was that he might be revealed to Israel" (see also John 11:51-52).

Hints of the Rapture

As we'll see in chapter 12, up to this time, the rapture was a mystery—meaning its details were not known until God revealed them to Paul. But as we look back, we can see Jesus hinting at the rapture before Paul ever knew there would be such a thing.

In John chapter 11 (in the context of the death of Lazarus), we find a conversation between Jesus and Martha about the death of her brother, Lazarus.

Martha was upset that Jesus had not come earlier to heal Lazarus before he died. In verses 25-26, Jesus said, "I am the resurrection and the life; the one who believes in Me will live, even if he dies, and everyone who lives and believes in Me will never die. Do you believe this?" (NASB).

Surely Jesus was speaking about salvation in general—that whoever believes in him would have eternal life. But I believe this statement was also a foreshadow of the rapture. Notice these two key details: first, that if someone dies in Christ, they will yet live (that is, they will be resurrected). And second, that if someone lives and believes in Jesus, they will never see death.

This follows the same two key details about the rapture as found in 1 Thessalonians 4:16-17, where we read,

> The Lord himself will come down from heaven, with a loud command, with the voice of the archangel and with the trumpet call of God, and the dead in Christ will rise first. After that, we who are still alive and are left will be caught up together with them in the clouds to meet the Lord in the air. And so we will be with the Lord forever.

We find further hints of the rapture in the Gospel of John when we get to chapter 14. In verses 1-3, we read, "Do not let your hearts be troubled. You believe in God; believe also in me. My Father's house has many rooms; if that were not so, would I have told you that I am going there to prepare a place for you? And if I go and prepare a place for you, I will come back and take you to be with me that you also may be where I am."

If you haven't done so previously, read John 14:1-3 again in light of 1 Thessalonians 4:16-17. Notice that in John 14, Jesus is not portrayed as coming all the way to earth, but he will receive us somewhere between heaven and earth. He will come back and "take" us so that we may be where he is.

ACTS

From a careful study of the "we" and "us" statements that appear in Acts (16:10-17; 20:5–21:18; 27:1–28:16), it is clear that the book was written by doctor Luke, who also wrote the Gospel that bears his name. It's even addressed to the same individual, Theophilus, and references the Gospel of Luke (Acts 1:1).

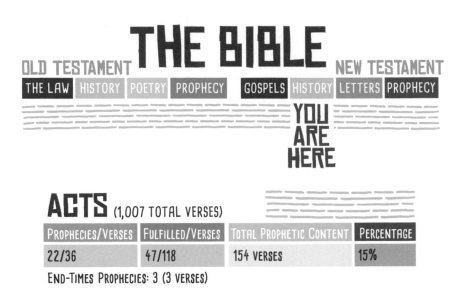

THE BIBLE

OLD TESTAMENT | NEW TESTAMENT

THE LAW | HISTORY | POETRY | PROPHECY | GOSPELS | HISTORY | LETTERS | PROPHECY

YOU
ARE
HERE

ACTS (1,007 TOTAL VERSES)

PROPHECIES/VERSES	FULFILLED/VERSES	TOTAL PROPHETIC CONTENT	PERCENTAGE
22/36	47/118	154 VERSES	15%

END-TIMES PROPHECIES: 3 (3 VERSES)

The arrival of the Holy Spirit on the day of Pentecost (Acts 2) served as a clear marker that a new era had arrived. The mysterious gap between the mountain peaks mentioned in Daniel 9 is now beginning to be revealed, which is consistent with what Jesus taught in his parables about the church age.

Another fascinating event recorded for us in Acts is the conversion of the first Gentiles (Acts 10). We'll discuss the theological import of that in the next chapter when we look at the book of Romans.

Other key events include the deaths of Ananias and Sapphira (chapter 5), the persecution and death of the first Christian martyr (chapters 6–7), the first wave of widespread persecution (chapter 8), the first African convert (chapter 8), Paul's powerful conversion experience (chapter 9), Peter's miraculous escape from prison (chapter 12), and Paul's three missionary journeys (chapters 13 to 21).

There are a few prophetically significant passages in Acts (including the recounting of God's past activities by Stephen in his sermon in Acts chapter 7, which led to his being the first martyr of the church age). In Acts 17:31, we read, "He has set a day when he will judge the world with justice by the man he has appointed. He has given proof of this to everyone by raising him from the dead."

That prophecy of future judgment (including the tribulation period and Jesus's rule during the millennial kingdom) reads like a messianic mission statement! From Genesis to the launch of the church, God's plan consistently displays the same themes and chronology. As we'll see, all of this sets the framework for the prophetic elements that appear in the rest of the New Testament—culminating in the all-important prophecies of the book of Revelation!

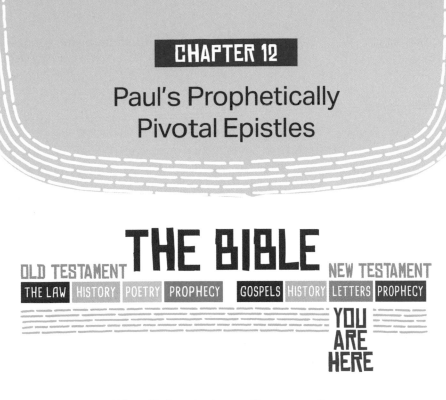

CHAPTER 12

Paul's Prophetically Pivotal Epistles

*When Christ, who is your life, appears, then
you also will appear with him in glory.*

—COLOSSIANS 3:4

The first 13 letters that follow the book of Acts were all written by Paul. They are as follows: Romans, 1 Corinthians, 2 Corinthians, Galatians, Ephesians, Philippians, Colossians, 1 Thessalonians, 2 Thessalonians, 1 Timothy, 2 Timothy, Titus, and Philemon. These letters cover a wide array of topics ranging from weighty theology, to church governing practices, to practical aspects of living out the Christian faith. Four of Paul's letters—Ephesians, Philippians, Colossians, and Philemon—are known as the prison epistles. He wrote them while under house arrest (AD 60–61) in Rome, awaiting trial.

All of Paul's letters except for Philemon contain prophetic content, and all of those—except for Galatians, Ephesians, and Philippians—include prophecies related to the end times. Among the nine letters that contain end-times prophecies, 1 and 2 Thessalonians are the most eschatological. The letter of

2 Thessalonians has the highest percentage of end-times prophetic content (36 percent).

Mystery Man

In Acts chapter 7, Saul (also known as Paul) oversaw and approved the killing of the first Christian martyr (verse 58). In Acts chapter 9, we read about Saul's active persecution of the believers in the early church. In the middle of his efforts, Saul was supernaturally knocked off his feet and heard the voice of Jesus. It appears Paul was instantly converted (verse 5). Talk about a 180!

In Galatians 1:13-24, Paul provides an autobiographical summary of his conversion:

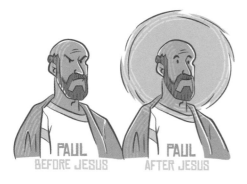

You have heard of my previous way of life in Judaism, how intensely I persecuted the church of God and tried to destroy it. I was advancing in Judaism beyond many of my own age among my people and was extremely zealous for the traditions of my fathers. But when God, who set me apart from my mother's womb and called me by his grace, was pleased to reveal his Son in me so that I might preach him among the Gentiles, my immediate response was not to consult any human being. I did not go up to Jerusalem to see those who were apostles before I was, but I went into Arabia. Later I returned to Damascus.

Then after three years, I went up to Jerusalem to get acquainted with Cephas and stayed with him fifteen days. I saw none of the other apostles—only James, the Lord's brother. I assure you before God that what I am writing you is no lie.

Then I went to Syria and Cilicia. I was personally unknown to the churches of Judea that are in Christ. They only heard the report: "The man who formerly persecuted us is now preaching the faith he once tried to destroy." And they praised God because of me.

It was likely that, during Paul's three-year soul-searching hiatus, he experienced something that no other apostle (except John with the book of Revelation) had experienced. Or if they had, they did not write about it. In 2 Corinthians 12:2-4, Paul, speaking of himself, wrote,

> I know a man in Christ who fourteen years ago was caught up to the third heaven. Whether it was in the body or out of the body I do not know—God knows. And I know that this man—whether in the body or apart from the body I do not know, but God knows—was caught up to paradise and heard inexpressible things, things that no one is permitted to tell.

Presumably, it was during that experience that Paul learned the details about the mystery of the rapture (and several other mysteries detailed in his letters and elsewhere in the New Testament). The theologian (and fellow illustrator) Clarence Larkin counted 11 such mysteries detailed in Paul's letters (8), described by Jesus (1), and found in Revelation (2).

In Scripture, a mystery is not something that can't be known. Rather, it is something that was not previously known until God revealed it. One of the primary mysteries shown to Paul was that of the rapture. Now that we know what the rapture is, we can see it hinted at in hindsight. But, prior to Paul's explanation of the mystery, nobody had a clue. When a mystery is revealed, it brings clarity to previous events and passages of Scripture. Now with the rapture clearly described, we better understand the resurrection, the ascension, Elijah and Enoch's mysterious departures, the nature of our future glorified spiritual bodies, and so much more.

In 1 Corinthians 15:51-52, Paul said, "Listen, I tell you a mystery: We will not all sleep, but we will all be changed—in a flash, in the twinkling of an eye, at the last trumpet. For the trumpet will sound, the dead will be raised imperishable, and we will be changed."

Then in 1 Thessalonians 4:13-18, Paul wrote,

> Brothers and sisters, we do not want you to be uninformed about those who sleep in death, so that you do not grieve like the rest of mankind, who have no hope. For we believe that Jesus died and rose again, and so we believe that God will bring with Jesus those who have fallen asleep in him. According to the Lord's word, we

tell you that we who are still alive, who are left until the coming of the Lord, will certainly not precede those who have fallen asleep. For the Lord himself will come down from heaven, with a loud command, with the voice of the archangel and with the trumpet call of God, and the dead in Christ will rise first. After that, we who are still alive and are left will be caught up together with them in the clouds to meet the Lord in the air. And so we will be with the Lord forever. Therefore encourage one another with these words.

Those are the two key rapture passages in Scripture (compare with John 11:25-26; 14:3). They provide crystal-clear details about the future event known as the rapture. Paul does not say anything about the overall end-times chronology here, but, as we'll see below, he does provide the chronology in his second letter to the Thessalonian church.

In any case, Paul—the mystery man—played a unique role in the early stages of the church age as he was used by God to take the gospel to the Gentiles. The ministry of this one man (through the strength and sovereignty of God, along with the help of many others), changed the trajectory of history from that time forward. Let's take a closer look at some of the prophetic sections of his letters.

ROMANS

ROMANS (433 TOTAL VERSES)			
PROPHECIES/VERSES	FULFILLED/VERSES	TOTAL PROPHETIC CONTENT	PERCENTAGE
26/44	17/42	86 VERSES	20%

END-TIMES PROPHECIES: 8 (45 VERSES/10%)

God's Abandonment Wrath

In Romans 1:18-32, we learn about a form of God's wrath that is already "being revealed" (verse 18). Theologians refer to this as God's abandonment wrath—as opposed to God's active wrath on earth, which will be poured out during the future tribulation period. God's abandonment wrath is his response to people's continual rejection of him. In essence, God gives nations what they are asking for. God is a gentleman and will not force his principles on anyone—even though his principles are designed for our protection. The sad reality is that when an individual or a nation keeps pushing God away, his protection leaves with his presence. The two go together.

The progression we read about in Romans 1:18-32 reveals that as people or nations reject God, he takes incremental steps away from them. Here, we see the prophetic principle that any nation that follows this pattern will end up in the same place. Any people who rebel against God corporately will go from the heights of power to internal collapse and eventual obscurity. This is a prophetic pattern, and it is the trajectory of our entire world as we approach the tribulation period.

That's exactly what happened with the collapse of the Roman Empire, and it's the same trajectory we've witnessed in the West over the past 100-plus years. The West leads much of the rest of the world, so we're seeing this pattern repeated on a global scale in our day. Here's the pattern:

> **Step 1:** Verse 20—creation points to a creator, which means people who don't acknowledge God have no excuse.
>
> **Step 2:** Verse 21—A society that knows the ways of God then fails to glorify and thank him damages their thinking.
>
> **Step 3:** Verse 22—People will think they are wiser than God but are actually fools.
>
> **Step 4:** Verse 23—They will worship man (humanism) and nature (environmentalism) instead of God.
>
> **Step 5:** Verse 24—This will result in a sexual revolution (delusional ideas impact behavior).
>
> **Step 6:** Verse 25—Truth will be exchanged for "a lie" and the worship of creation instead of the Creator (that is, evolution/naturalism).
>
> **Step 7:** Verses 26-27—This results in a homosexual revolution (a further drift from God's created order).
>
> **Step 8:** Verses 28-30—Society will be given over to a depraved mind, which results in widespread chaos and every form of evil.

Here is an important reminder as we consider the abandonment judgment of Romans 1: If indeed we are in the latter stages of this judgment (and I believe we are), our calling as believers is still the same as it has always been. We are called to love people, live godly lives (be in the world but not of it—1 John 2:15), and share the gospel with a lost and dying world. Matthew 28:19-20 provides our clear marching orders from Jesus: "Go and make disciples of all nations, baptizing them in the name of the Father and of the Son and of the Holy Spirit, and teaching them to obey everything I have commanded you. And surely I am with you always, to the very end of the age."

God's Continued Plan for Israel

As you'll recall, throughout this book I have pointed out key prophetic passages that demonstrate the clear fact that God is not finished with Israel or the Jewish people. The church has not replaced Israel, but has been grafted in (Romans 11:17-24). This is an admittedly confusing topic if you have never studied it before. In fact, it is another one of the mysteries revealed to Paul. In Ephesians 3:6, we read, "This mystery is that through the gospel the Gentiles are heirs together with Israel, members together of one body, and sharers together in the promise in Christ Jesus."

So one of the mysteries revealed to Paul was that God has a plan to merge his chosen people—the Israelites—with non-Jewish believers from all over the world. This flies in the face of replacement theology, which teaches that the church has replaced Israel in God's plan. Simply put, God is not done with the Jewish people. In fact, Paul spends three full chapters in Romans explaining this mysterious merging of the two.

In Romans chapters 9–11, Paul goes into great detail about how Gentiles are grafted in to God's plans for the Jewish people. We are told that during the church age, the Jewish people will experience a partial hardening of their hearts until the full number of Gentiles comes in (Romans 11:25), after which a full remnant of the Jewish people will be saved (Romans 11:26). As we study specific prophecies in the Old Testament and the book of Revelation, it becomes clear that this moment when all Israel will be saved will occur at the end of the tribulation period. A protected remnant of Jewish people (Revelation 12:6) will call on the one whom they pierced (Zechariah 12:10) and say, "Blessed is he who comes in the name of the Lord" (Matthew 23:39).

It is important to remember that the future tribulation period is Daniel's seventieth week (Daniel 9). During this time span, the focus will be entirely on Israel and the Jewish people. The Lord will judge the world and win back his chosen people, who will finally realize that Jesus is indeed their Messiah.

Scripture clearly states that each individual person (Jew or Gentile) must make a personal decision to accept Christ for salvation, and that God's prophetic promises to Israel and the Jewish people still remain and will be fulfilled during the future millennial kingdom. Here are some select verses from Romans chapter 11 (after the buildup in chapters 9–10) that clearly highlight the fact that the church has not replaced Israel.

11:1—"Did God reject his people? By no means!"

11:11—"Again I ask: Did they [Israel] stumble so as to fall beyond recovery? Not at all!"

11:12—"If their [Israel's] transgression means riches for the world, and their loss means riches for the Gentiles, how much greater riches will their full inclusion bring!"

11:15—"If their [Israel's] rejection [of Christ] brought reconciliation to the world [because the gospel then went out to the Gentiles], what will their acceptance be but life from the dead?"

11:18—"Do not consider yourself [the church/Gentiles] to be superior to those other branches [Israel/Jews]. If you do, consider this: You do not support the root, but the root [Israel] supports you [the church]."

11:25-27—"I do not want you to be ignorant of this mystery, brothers and sisters [that is, the church], so that you may not be conceited: Israel has experienced a hardening in part until the full number of the Gentiles has come in [that is, until all church-age Gentile believers have accepted Christ], and in this way all Israel will be saved. As it is written: 'The deliverer will come from Zion [Jerusalem]; he will turn godlessness away from Jacob. And this is my covenant with them when I take away their sins.'"

This teaching that the church has not replaced Israel—as stated in Romans 9–11—is often overlooked by believers, yet it gives clear evidence that God still has future plans for his chosen people. In fact, Paul sets up this key point in the opening chapter of Romans, where he wrote, "I am not ashamed of the gospel, because it is the power of God that brings salvation to everyone who believes: first to the Jew, then to the Gentile" (verse 16). From there onward, Paul unpacks the theology of salvation and the truths of God's continued relationships with Israel and the church.

More True Now

If truth is truth, how can something become truer? Well, read the following passage, and you will see what I mean. In Romans 13:11-12, Paul wrote, "Do this, understanding the present time: The hour has already come for you to wake up from your slumber, because our salvation is nearer now than when we first believed. The night is nearly over; the day is almost here. So let us put aside the deeds of darkness and put on the armor of light."

Paul said that our salvation is nearer now than it was when we first believed. That was true for believers of his day, and it is true for us. The return of the Lord is closer than it has ever been. These verses are truer now than they were in Paul's day!

There will be no other ages before the Lord returns. This is it. The church age will end with the rapture, and the seven-year tribulation will transition into the millennial kingdom.

1 AND 2 CORINTHIANS

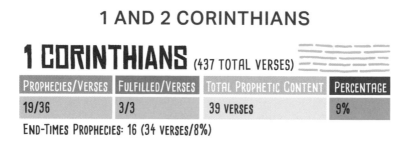

1 CORINTHIANS (437 TOTAL VERSES)

PROPHECIES/VERSES	FULFILLED/VERSES	TOTAL PROPHETIC CONTENT	PERCENTAGE
19/36	3/3	39 VERSES	9%

END-TIMES PROPHECIES: 16 (34 VERSES/8%)

2 CORINTHIANS (257 TOTAL VERSES)

PROPHECIES/VERSES	FULFILLED/VERSES	TOTAL PROPHETIC CONTENT	PERCENTAGE
9/16	1/2	18 VERSES	7%

END-TIMES PROPHECIES: 9 (9 VERSES)

In addition to the discovery of the mystery of the rapture found in 1 Corinthians (discussed above), there are also other prophetic themes and sections in Paul's letters to the Corinthians. One of them is the judgment seat of Christ.

As believers in Christ, you and I will appear before his judgment seat—also known as the bema seat (2 Corinthians 5:10). We learn more about this future event in 1 Corinthians 3:10-15, where Paul wrote,

> By the grace God has given me, I laid a foundation as a wise builder, and someone else is building on it. But each one should build with care. For no one can lay any foundation other than the one already laid, which is Jesus Christ. If anyone builds on this foundation using gold, silver, costly stones, wood, hay or straw, their work will be shown for what it is, because the Day will bring it to light. It will be revealed with fire, and the fire will test the quality of each person's work. If what has been built survives, the builder will receive a reward. If it is burned up, the builder will suffer loss but yet will be saved—even though only as one escaping through the flames.

There are a few important things to note in this passage. First, we will not be judged with regard to our salvation. We will already be in heaven. This is a judgment for rewards. No one is going to watch a movie of our life that shows all our sins. Jesus paid for our sins on the cross. The picture here is that of giving out medals at the Olympics. We will gain rewards for our service to the Lord after our salvation. God will reward us based on our faithfulness and motives, not our outward actions that everyone sees.

Some of these rewards involve responsibilities in the millennial kingdom, and some of them are eternal rewards. We can't even imagine what these rewards will be, for we are currently limited by our fallen nature and our natural bodies and minds.

Trusted Bible teachers believe that the bema seat, or the judgment seat of Christ, will occur in heaven right after the rapture, while the tribulation is taking place on the earth.

GALATIANS (149 TOTAL VERSES)

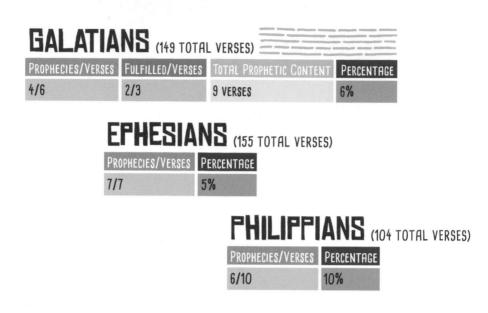

Prophecies/Verses	Fulfilled/Verses	Total Prophetic Content	Percentage
4/6	2/3	9 VERSES	6%

EPHESIANS (155 TOTAL VERSES)

Prophecies/Verses	Percentage
7/7	5%

PHILIPPIANS (104 TOTAL VERSES)

Prophecies/Verses	Percentage
6/10	10%

COLOSSIANS

COLOSSIANS (95 TOTAL VERSES)

Prophecies/Verses	Percentage
3/3	3%

END-TIMES PROPHECIES: 2 (2 VERSES)

One of the three clear prophetic passages in Colossians is 3:24-25, which reads, "You know that you will receive an inheritance from the Lord as a reward. It is the Lord Christ you are serving. Anyone who does wrong will be repaid for their wrongs, and there is no favoritism."

These verses serve as a good practical reminder for us to shift our focus from the struggles and injustices of this world to our promised glorious future, where God sets all accounts straight and where we get to enjoy an eternal, heavenly inheritance!

1 AND 2 THESSALONIANS

1 THESSALONIANS (89 TOTAL VERSES)

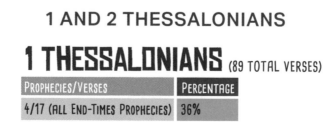

Prophecies/Verses	Percentage
4/17 (ALL END-TIMES PROPHECIES)	36%

2 THESSALONIANS (47 TOTAL VERSES)

PROPHECIES/VERSES	PERCENTAGE
17/134	64%

MESSIANIC: 1 (8 VERSES) | END-TIMES PROPHECIES: 6 (36 VERSES/17%)

In 1 Thessalonians, Paul reminds his readers of his personal example as he lives out the faith in front of them. Then he urges them to persevere through trials and struggles. He also comforts them regarding believers who have died. First Thessalonians 4:13-18 is one of the two key rapture passages in the New Testament (the other is found in 1 Corinthians 15:51-52, as highlighted after the opening of this chapter). I won't rehash the amazing truth of the mystery we now know as the rapture, but there are other vital end-times prophecies found in Paul's letters to the Thessalonians as well.

The two letters to the Thessalonians were probably among the first that Paul wrote. This is an important detail because it gives us a glimpse of what Paul considered key content for his "New Believers 101" class, so to speak.

What we find is that new believers in the early church were taught eschatology, or truths about the end times. They learned about the rapture, the tribulation period, the antichrist, and the return of Christ. As mentioned above, out of all of Paul's 13 letters, the ones to the Thessalonians included the most teachings about the end times.

In short, the resurrection and rapture of the church completes our salvation, which began at the moment we believed in Christ as our Savior and Lord. In that moment, we were saved (past tense) from the penalty of our sin. As we grow in Christ awaiting his return, we are being saved (present tense) from the power of sin. At the rapture, believers who are alive on earth will be saved (future tense) from the presence of sin. The rapture of the church and the return of Christ are key aspects to our salvation as believers.

The main reason for Paul's second letter was to clear up some confusion (or possibly even some intentional misrepresentation by someone) regarding the timing of the future tribulation period—known as the Day of the Lord. Due to the persecution the Thessalonian believers were facing, someone had convinced them that they had already entered the Day of the Lord (2:1-2). Paul assured them this was not the case, and said that the departure (which could refer to spiritual apostasy or physical removal via the rapture) and the revealing of the antichrist had to occur first (2:3).

Paul also assured his readers that the antichrist could not be revealed until the Holy Spirit-indwelled church (called the restrainer here in this passage) was removed (2:6-8). In other words, the antichrist and the evil he brings will be restrained or held back until the rapture occurs. On the flip side, God's active judgment (that is, the Day of the Lord) will also be restrained until Christ takes his bride (the church—see Ephesians 5:23) out of the way of judgment (1 Thessalonians 5:9; Revelation 3:10).

The Man of Lawlessness

In 2 Thessalonians 2, where we learn of the restrainer—or the Holy Spirit—being removed, we discover that the antichrist can't be revealed to the world until after the Spirit is removed via the rapture. By the way, it's not that the Holy Spirit won't be active or present (he is omnipotent and omnipresent), but that his work through the salt and light of the church will be gone. Think about it: When the rapture occurs, it will be the first time since the birth of the church that there will be no true Christians on the earth. There will be no righteous influence or Holy Spirit-guided decisions about what to do in the aftermath of the rapture. Evil will fill the void and tip the scales.

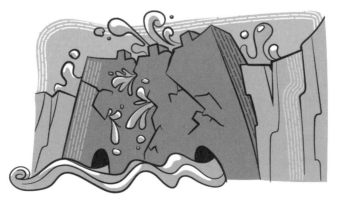

In 2 Thessalonians 2:7-10, we read,

> The secret power of lawlessness is already at work; but the one who now holds it back will continue to do so till he is taken out of the way. And then the lawless one will be revealed, whom the Lord Jesus will overthrow with the breath of his mouth and destroy by the splendor of his coming. The coming of the lawless one will be in accordance with how Satan works. He will use all sorts of displays of power through signs and wonders that serve the lie, and all the ways that wickedness deceives those who are perishing.

Active Waiting

Paul also encouraged the Thessalonians to remain busy while they waited for Christ's return (3:6-12). Knowing the Lord is coming soon should not lead us to stop working. Rather, it should motivate us to work hard until the day he calls us home—either by rapture or by death.

1 AND 2 TIMOTHY

1 TIMOTHY (113 TOTAL VERSES)

Prophecies/Verses	Percentage
3/6	5%

END-TIMES PROPHECIES: 2 (5 VERSES)

2 TIMOTHY (83 TOTAL VERSES)

Prophecies/Verses	Percentage
8/14 (ALL END-TIMES PROPHECIES)	17%

End-Times Conditions

Paul's second letter to Timothy highlights two key end-time conditions: lawlessness and apostasy.

In 2 Timothy chapter 3:1-5, we read the following description about the last days:

> Mark this: There will be terrible times in the last days. People will be lovers of themselves, lovers of money, boastful, proud, abusive, disobedient to their parents, ungrateful, unholy,

without love, unforgiving, slanderous, without self-control, brutal, not lovers of the good, treacherous, rash, conceited, lovers of pleasure rather than lovers of God—having a form of godliness but denying its power.

Then in verse 13, we're told that "evildoers and impostors will go from bad to worse, deceiving and being deceived."

As for apostasy, in 2 Timothy 4:3-4, we're warned that "the time will come when people will not put up with sound doctrine. Instead, to suit their own desires, they will gather around them a great number of teachers to say what their itching ears want to hear. They will turn their ears away from the truth and turn aside to myths."

Fortunately, we're given some instructions on how to deal with the apostasy. In verse 5, we read, "Keep your head in all situations, endure hardship, do the work of an evangelist, discharge all the duties of your ministry."

The Crown of Righteousness

Some of the eternal rewards we'll be given at the judgment seat of Christ will be what the Bible describes as crowns. One such crown is mentioned in 2 Timothy 4:8—a crown for those who long for Christ's appearing: "There is in store for me the crown of righteousness, which the Lord, the righteous Judge, will award to me on that day—and not only to me, but also to all who have longed for his appearing."

You would think that all believers would long for Christ's return, but in our day, many have become so comfortable with the world that they no longer are eager for the Lord to come back. But the remnant that does wait with eager anticipation will do so more and more as the world gets darker.

In the next chapter, we'll discuss crowns a bit more, and I'll share details about the five crowns that are mentioned in the New Testament.

TITUS (46 TOTAL VERSES)

PROPHECIES/VERSES	PERCENTAGE
2/2	4%

END-TIMES PROPHECIES: 1 (1 VERSE)

PHILEMON (25 TOTAL VERSES)

PROPHECIES/VERSES	PERCENTAGE
0/0	0%

Now that we have seen the richly prophetic nature of Paul's letters, let's take a brief look at the rest of the New Testament epistles.

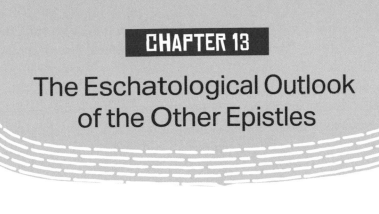

CHAPTER 13

The Eschatological Outlook of the Other Epistles

*Bear in mind that our Lord's patience means salvation,
just as our dear brother Paul also wrote you
with the wisdom that God gave him.*

—2 PETER 3:15

HEBREWS

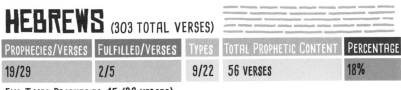

HEBREWS (303 TOTAL VERSES)				
PROPHECIES/VERSES	FULFILLED/VERSES	TYPES	TOTAL PROPHETIC CONTENT	PERCENTAGE
19/29	2/5	9/22	56 VERSES	18%

END-TIMES PROPHECIES: 15 (28 VERSES)

ased on the title of the book and the contents, Hebrews was most likely written by a Jewish believer to other Jewish believers. Of course, because of its inclusion in the canon of Scripture, it was also written to all Gentile believers as well. The primary thrust of the book is that Jesus is the fulfillment of prophecy and is superior in every way, including the law—and before the law. Specifically, Christ is greater than the prophets, (1:1-3), the angels (1:4–2:18), Moses (3), Joshua (4:1-13), the priests (4:14–7:28), the tabernacle (8:1-5), the old covenant (8:6–9:22), and the animal sacrifices (9:23–10:39).

The last three chapters serve as the crescendo of the book. Chapter 11 is the great faith chapter that recounts examples of faithful believers. It reads like a powerful halftime speech. Then chapters 12 and 13 challenge believers to live out their faith and explain many specific ways in which to do just that.

In terms of prophecy, one could argue that a large portion of the book contains prophetic typology because the entire book connects the Old Testament foreshadows of the Messiah to their New Testament fulfillments. But for the sake of being careful, I chose to include only what seemed to be clear and specific prophecy. So the 18 percent that I catalogued could potentially be higher. J. Barton Payne, in his *Encyclopedia of Bible Prophecy* (page 572), cites 45 percent of Hebrews as prophecy because of the typology. I do believe his determination is 100 percent valid, but as I mentioned in chapter 1, I intentionally took a conservative approach and catalogued only prophecies and types that are referenced elsewhere in the Bible or are so compelling even a skeptic would have to take notice. With all of that said, here are a few handpicked prophetic passages from Hebrews for you to consider.

Not Done with the Jewish People

At this point in the book, I'm sure it will sound redundant for me to say that from Genesis to Revelation, it is clear that God is not done with the Jewish people. The reason I keep bringing up this consistent theme is for the simple reason that it is a consistent theme. That sentence is intentionally redundant to underscore the point I'm making.

Here is yet another case in point. In Hebrews 8:8-13, we read,

> The days are coming, declares the Lord, when I will make a new covenant with the people of Israel and with the people of Judah. It will not be like the covenant I made with their ancestors when I took them by the hand to lead them out of Egypt, because they did not remain faithful to my covenant, and I turned away from them, declares the Lord. This is the covenant I will establish with

the people of Israel after that time, declares the Lord. I will put my laws in their minds and write them on their hearts. I will be their God, and they will be my people. No longer will they teach their neighbor, or say to one another, "Know the Lord," because they will all know me, from the least of them to the greatest. For I will forgive their wickedness and will remember their sins no more. By calling this covenant "new," he has made the first one obsolete; and what is obsolete and outdated will soon disappear.

Jesus fulfilled everything that the law pointed to. Read the passage above in light of Romans 11:26, where Paul plainly states that "all Israel will be saved." Notice in Hebrews 8:11 that it states, "They will all know me, from the least of them to the greatest." I'm no biblical scholar, but I looked up the Hebrew and Greek words translated "all." You know what it means? *All.* All Israel will be saved. There is coming a day when all the people of Israel will recognize Jesus is their Messiah. When we put the puzzle pieces of the end times together, we see this will occur at the end of the tribulation—and this is the primary purpose of the tribulation: to draw the Jewish people to the Messiah. At the risk of additional redundancy, the future tribulation period is the seventieth week mentioned in Daniel 9—which is 100 percent specifically about the Jewish people (verse 24).

The Purpose of the Second Coming

Some verses in Scripture do an amazing job of distilling everything down to a core meaning. Like a mission statement, brand message, or core value, sometimes the arrangement of an economy of words serves to clarify everything related to a given topic.

This happens in Hebrews 9:28, where we read, "Christ was sacrificed once to take away the sins of many; and he will appear a second time, not to bear sin, but to bring salvation to those who are waiting for him."

I love the profound simplicity of that verse. It does not get more prophetically poignant than that. We understand the clear reason for both advents. I also love the fact that the second coming statement can apply to both the church (at the rapture) and the Jewish believers at the second coming (at Christ's physical return to earth).

Timely Text for Today

Hebrews 10:23-25 reads,

> Let us hold unswervingly to the hope we profess, for he who promised is faithful. And let us consider how we may spur one another on toward love and good deeds, not giving up meeting together, as some are in the habit of doing, but encouraging one another—and all the more as you see the Day approaching.

There is so much instruction here that is more practical for Christians today than at any other time in history. Not only are we closer to the Day of the Lord, but we clearly see it approaching. The tribulation casts its shadow forward. When COVID-19 was unleashed, many churches shut down for long periods of time. When governmental overreach and church leaders work in a way that is contrary to the clear teaching in Scripture that we are to gather together, these verses from Hebrews take on heightened meaning. We are not to stop assembling together "all the more" as we "see the Day approaching."

From this we learn that even in the first century, believers were tempted to give up meeting together. In our day, we need to resist this temptation all the more. Key to us holding the line and sticking to Scripture's game plan is the fact that God is faithful (verse 23)! Anchoring ourselves to that single fact helps us to "hold unswervingly to the hope we profess."

A 1,400-Year Object Lesson

In Hebrews 10:19-20, we read, "Therefore, brothers and sisters, since we have confidence to enter the Most Holy Place by the blood of Jesus, by a new and living way opened for us through the curtain, that is, his body."

Just as Jesus's body was torn and his blood sacrificially shed for our salvation, the three-inch thick curtain separating the Holy of Holies from the rest of the temple was torn in two from top to bottom when Jesus died on the cross (Matthew 27:51). Accompanied by an earthquake, this literal historical event symbolically showed that God did it all. He reached down from above and tore away the barrier between himself and man. Salvation was a top-down sacrifice secured for us by God alone. *Grace*—one of the world's single most powerful words—is highlighted here in Hebrews in all of its beauty.

The New Jerusalem

In Revelation 21, we get the most complete description of the New Jerusalem that is found in the Bible, but we find several references to it here in the book of Hebrews (11:10; 12:22-24; 13:14). Some Bible scholars believe the New Jerusalem exists right now and is where Jesus is building our custom-built living spaces (John 14:2-3).

In Revelation, we discover that the New Jerusalem is a 1,400-mile square that will descend from heaven to earth when God creates the new heavens and new earth. You can read all about this in Revelation 21. In Hebrews 13:14, we're offered a brief comment about this otherworldly city: "Here we do not have an enduring city, but we are looking for the city that is to come."

JAMES

JAMES (108 TOTAL VERSES)

PROPHECIES/VERSES	PERCENTAGE
4/6 (ALL END-TIMES PROPHECIES)	6%

The book of James is a very practical epistle (letter). While Paul emphasized grace (Galatians/ Romans, etc.) and the fact that works can't make us right with God, James emphasized works—not as a means to salvation, but as a result of salvation (2:14-26). The reformer Martin Luther rejected James as being an official part of the biblical canon because he thought James was contradicting Paul, but James was not. James was merely highlighting the fact that real faith plays itself out through real action. He wasn't arguing for faith *plus* works. Rather, he was arguing for a faith *that* works.

James also discussed other topics in his letter. He talked about how to endure trials (1:2-18), tame the tongue (3:1-12), ask God for wisdom (3:13-18), and avoid becoming worldly (4:1-17).

As for prophetic content, anything found in James related to the end-times features basic aspects of the Lord's return. But there is one verse that provides some new information related to another potential reward for the believer— the crown of life.

I noted in the previous chapter the crown of righteousness, which will be given to all who long for the Lord's return. Here in James, we discover another crown—one for those who persevere. All told, the New Testament mentions five crowns, which are depicted in the chart below.

FIVE CROWNS

- 👑 **THE IMPERISHABLE CROWN** (1 CORINTHIANS 9:24-25)
- 👑 **THE CROWN OF REJOICING** (1 THESSALONIANS 2:19)
- 👑 **THE CROWN OF RIGHTEOUSNESS** (2 TIMOTHY 4:8)
- 👑 **THE CROWN OF GLORY** (1 PETER 5:4)
- 👑 **THE CROWN OF LIFE** (JAMES 1:12; REVELATION 2:10)

In James 1:12, we read, "Blessed is the one who perseveres under trial because, having stood the test, that person will receive the crown of life that the Lord has promised to those who love him."

Talk about practical application! What believer has not gone through trials and tests that require great perseverance? To varying degrees, we've all had to endure such. Knowing there will be rewards for our struggles and that the Lord sees every trial we go through should bring us great comfort and assist us in persevering under pressure.

The crown of life is also mentioned in Revelation 2, where it relates to various forms of severe persecution. First Corinthians 15:40-42 seems to indicate there will be varying degrees of glory associated with our future rewards. Given what we know about God's character and fairness, it would make sense that a martyr would likely obtain a more glorious crown of life than a Christian who suffered less yet still persevered through trials.

1 PETER

1 PETER (105 TOTAL VERSES)

PROPHECIES/VERSES	FULFILLED/VERSES	TOTAL PROPHETIC CONTENT	PERCENTAGE
9/13	2/4	17 VERSES	16%

END-TIMES PROPHECIES: 7 (11 VERSES)

Peter wrote this letter from Rome (which he called Babylon to avoid any trouble from the Romans) just a few years before he was martyred (ca. AD 67). He addressed it to the "exiles scattered throughout the provinces" (1:1). Scholars differ (at least in the various commentaries I read) on whether this letter was directed to Jewish believers, Gentile believers, or both.

In any case, Peter links his readers to Israel of old during the nation's first period of dispersion.

The believers Peter wrote to were facing tough times of persecution as they were trying to live out their faith in a hostile, pagan culture. This was also just before Nero's great persecution of believers started in AD 64, and a few years before Rome destroyed Jerusalem in AD 70. Peter encouraged his readers to persevere through suffering and to give an answer or reason for their beliefs when asked (3:15). He also assured them that God was fully aware of all that they were facing—and that their suffering here is only for "a little while" (5:10).

There are a couple of prophetic passages in 1 Peter I'd like to highlight. One of them appears in the closing chapter. The other is 1 Peter 4:7-8, where he wrote, "The end of all things is near. Therefore be alert and of sober mind so that you may pray. Above all, love each other deeply, because love covers over a multitude of sins."

Peter had a long and mature view of the Lord's return. In light of eternity, he knew the end of all things would happen soon. The older I get, the more I realize how short life is. Eternity is near. Two or three million years from now, the entire history of planet Earth will seem but a moment. With that in mind, Peter encourages us to be sober-minded, prayerful, and loving.

2 PETER

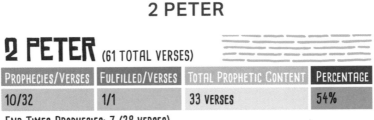

2 PETER (61 TOTAL VERSES)

PROPHECIES/VERSES	FULFILLED/VERSES	TOTAL PROPHETIC CONTENT	PERCENTAGE
10/32	1/1	33 VERSES	54%

END-TIMES PROPHECIES: 7 (28 VERSES)

This second letter from Peter contains his last-known recorded words before his martyrdom. He seems to know that his time was short (1:15). He reassures his readers that he was an eyewitness to the events of the life of Christ (1:16) and reminds his readers (including us) that even though not all believers will have seen Christ during his first coming, that we have "the prophetic message as something completely reliable" (1:19).

In other words, God's proven track record of fulfilling prophecy is so reliable that we can rest assured that all prophecy—including the return of Christ and the culmination of all things—will be fulfilled just as the Holy Spirit predicted through human prophets (1:21). Other key prophetic themes in 2 Peter include false teachers and scoffing in the last days.

False Teachers in Last Days

In 2 Peter 2:1-3 we read,

There were also false prophets among the people, just as there will be false teachers among you. They will secretly introduce destructive heresies, even denying the sovereign Lord who bought them— bringing swift destruction on themselves. Many will follow their depraved conduct and will bring the way of truth into disrepute. In their greed these teachers will exploit you with fabricated stories. Their condemnation has long been hanging over them, and their destruction has not been sleeping.

The proliferation of false teaching is a major end-time sign. Our generation has seen the great end-time falling away. Europe was once the hub of Christianity. It has since grown so apostate the church has, for the most part, given way to secularism, the occult, and more recently, Islam. America is following in hot pursuit. In many circles and denominations, "destructive heresies" have been introduced and are spreading.

Scoffers Will Scoff

Another problem that will arise during the last-days is scoffing. In 2 Peter 3:3-7, we read,

Above all, you must understand that in the last days scoffers will come, scoffing and following their own evil desires. They will say, "Where is this 'coming' he promised? Ever since our ancestors died, everything goes on as it has since the beginning of creation." But they deliberately forget that long ago by God's word the heavens came into being and the earth was formed out of water and by water. By these waters also the world of that time was deluged and destroyed. By the same word the present heavens and earth are reserved for fire, being kept for the day of judgment and destruction of the ungodly.

Notice that the scoffing will be directed toward creation, the flood of Noah's day, and the second coming. Those are three key aspects of the biblical narrative that are undermined by secular culture today. The belief in a literal six-day creation, the flood of Noah's day, and the future return of Christ are mocked and viewed as myths by many in our culture. Sadly, even within many churches, the biblical accounts of these subjects are taught as symbols or allegory, not literal truth.

1, 2, AND 3 JOHN

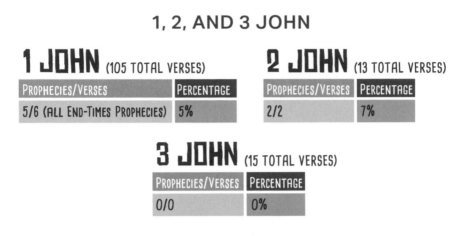

1 JOHN (105 TOTAL VERSES)

PROPHECIES/VERSES	PERCENTAGE
5/6 (ALL END-TIMES PROPHECIES)	5%

2 JOHN (13 TOTAL VERSES)

PROPHECIES/VERSES	PERCENTAGE
2/2	7%

3 JOHN (15 TOTAL VERSES)

PROPHECIES/VERSES	PERCENTAGE
0/0	0%

Dear children, this is the last hour; and as you have heard that the antichrist is coming, even now many antichrists have come. This is how we know it is the last hour.

—1 JOHN 2:18

The aged John—some 55-plus years after the events of Jesus's life—wrote this series of letters from Ephesus. First John seems to have been intended for believers all over Asia Minor, whereas 2 John was addressed to "the lady chosen by God and to her children" (verse 1—either a reference to the church/bride of Christ, an actual believing woman and her children whom John knew, or to Jesus's mother, whom John promised to care for as his own in John 19:25-27). And 3 John was addressed to John's friend Gaius (verse 1).

First John is full of contrasts (light and dark, love of God versus love of the world, children of God versus children of the devil, etc.), and, along with 2 and 3 John, was written before the widespread persecution by Domitian, which began in AD 95 (and led to John's exile to the isle of Patmos, where he wrote his final book, Revelation). We'll spend all of chapter 14 on John's book of Revelation.

JUDE

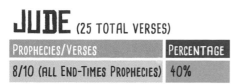

JUDE (25 TOTAL VERSES)

PROPHECIES/VERSES	PERCENTAGE
8/10 (ALL END-TIMES PROPHECIES)	40%

Jude provides a strong admonition for believers to carefully guard the fundamental original truths of the faith as well as false teachers and apostasy. He used examples from Scripture (and some from intertestamental period works) to make his point and highlighted the subversive nature of false teachers who secretly infiltrate the church to undermine truth.

Jude connected the trend of apostasy in his day with last-days events, during which apostasy will greatly increase. Jude pointed out traits that are usually associated with false teachers, including immorality, pride, greed, and divisiveness. Jude is only one chapter in length but is densely packed with Old Testament references, theology, practical advice for churches, and a strong challenge to "contend for the faith" (verse 3).

Jude also wrote on the themes of scoffing and false teachers in the last days. In verses 18-19, we read, "In the last times there will be scoffers who will follow their own ungodly desires. These are the people who divide you, who follow mere natural instincts and do not have the Spirit."

So, Jude specifically stated that in the last days, false teachers will infiltrate churches and introduce scoffing, division, cultural pragmatism, and Holy-Spiritless activity. Do we see any of these problems today? All of them line up with the characteristics visible in the end-time Laodicean church, which we'll examine in the next chapter. They also line up with what the New Testament says about the great end-time falling away.

All this dovetails into our next chapter, which brings us to the incredible prophetic climax of the Bible—the book of Revelation!

CHAPTER 14

Wildly Relevant Revelation

THE BIBLE

OLD TESTAMENT | NEW TESTAMENT

THE LAW | HISTORY | POETRY | PROPHECY | GOSPELS | HISTORY | LETTERS | PROPHECY

YOU
ARE
HERE

Blessed is the one who reads aloud the words of this prophecy, and blessed are those who hear it and take to heart what is written in it, because the time is near.

—REVELATION 1:3

REVELATION (404 TOTAL VERSES)

PROPHECIES/VERSES	PERCENTAGE
64/353 (ALL END-TIMES PROPHECIES)	87% (*OR 74%)

(*I INCLUDED CH. 2-3 [29 AND 22 VERSES]. NOT ALL SCHOLARS AGREE. SEE INFO BELOW.)

The one book most Christians usually think of when they hear the word *prophecy* is the book of Revelation. Unfortunately, it is also the one book many Christians tend to avoid. One reason many believers in our day do not read—much less study—this book is that it does not seem practical or relevant to their daily reality. But nothing could be further from the truth. The book of Revelation has some of the most wildly relevant application for believers of all ages—especially in our day! I say wild because there is a staggering amount of truly wild and miraculous prophecies in the book. And I say relevant because the events of the tribulation are casting their shadows ahead, and these prophecies seem to be on the near horizon.

Another reason people give for avoiding the book of Revelation is that it is too complicated. Contrary to popular belief, however, Revelation is not all that complicated, but the enemy has convinced people that it is so that they won't study it. Many people I talk with seem to think Revelation is too complex to understand, or that it is irrelevant, divisive, or just plain confusing. People are often surprised to learn that Revelation is the only book of the Bible that promises a blessing to those who read it. It's also the primary source of information about Satan's ultimate defeat and our ultimate victory. It's no wonder that the enemy does his best to discourage God's people from reading this amazing book.

The structure of Revelation is straightforward and simple. We are provided with this information in the first chapter. In Revelation 1:19, Christ tells John, "Write, therefore, what you have seen, what is now and what will take place later." Here we have the outline for the book of Revelation:

1. Things you have seen (glorified Christ in heaven, 1:12–18)

2. Things that are (direction to the seven churches, chapters 2–3)

3. Things that will take place later (future/tribulation/kingdom/ eternity, chapters 4–22)

There are also specific phrases throughout Revelation that demonstrate it is written primarily in chronological order—phrases like "after this," "when he had opened the seventh seal," "the seven last plagues," and "after these things." These are time-oriented sequential phrases, and there is a natural progression and buildup of events as we make our way through the book. We even find that the seal, trumpet, and bowl judgments are each numbered in order, from one through seven.

The only section that is not in chronological order is chapters 10–14. These are parenthetical or overview chapters. They provide more context for some of the broad themes and extended events of the tribulation period. They almost serve like an intermission in the middle of the book. After the seal and trumpet judgments, John paused to provide more context and details, and to let you catch your breath. Then he returned to the chronological sequence in chapter 15 with the bowl judgments.

RECAPPING THE OLD TESTAMENT

John assumed his readers would be familiar with the Old Testament. In fact, Revelation is a distinctly Jewish book. In it we find all kinds of Jewish symbolism, two Jewish witnesses, 144,000 Jewish evangelists, and the world's attention centered on Israel and Jerusalem during the end times. In Revelation's 404 verses, there are more than 800 references or allusions to the Old Testament! Hopefully you have read this book up to this point and are therefore already acquainted with the prophecies and some of the symbolism of the Old Testament.

The symbolism in Revelation is solved either by reading the immediate context in which it appears, or by cross-referencing passages from the Old Testament. Many Bible expositors teach what is known as "the law of first mention." To understand the doctrines or symbols used in Revelation, you must find the first place in Scripture that doctrine or symbol was mentioned. The first appearance of a teaching or symbol often provides tremendous insight into how it is to be understood later in Scripture. Cross-referencing all the uses of a key word or term will also help you to build upon a doctrine's or symbol's first mention.

This approach allows us to interpret scriptural content by using Scripture itself, instead of interpreting Scripture based on outside sources or our own thoughts and ideas. If God is the author of the Bible, we should expect to find a cohesiveness within it—and we do. The law of first mention, and the principle of interpreting Scripture with Scripture, both bear out a divine unity in the Bible as it relates to numbers, symbols, doctrines, names, places, and many other details. Using the law of first mention—and interpreting Scripture with Scripture—when studying Revelation helps to bring great clarity to most of the book's symbolic content.

THE DIFFERENT VIEWS OF THE BOOK OF REVELATION

Today, unity in the church is needed more than ever. We must unite around the fundamentals of the faith and avoid dividing over secondary issues. That said, handling biblical teaching and theology accurately is important, so it's good for us to be diligent as we seek to understand Scripture.

There are various views about the timing of key events related to the end times, and we will look at the most common views here. I have good friends who love the Lord who hold to different views than I do. Our differing end-times views are not a salvation issue, but there is really only one truth about any matter, so by necessity, we can't all be correct. The most important thing is that, as much as possible, we allow God's truth to guide our end-times theology—not our personal biases or preconceived notions.

I believe a consistent, literal approach to interpreting Scripture (which, of course, allows for clear figures of speech and poetic language) from Genesis 1:1 to Revelation 22:21 will logically and methodically lead one to conclude that it presents a clear, basic order of events defined loosely as pretribulation premillennialism. That is a fancy way of saying, "The rapture will occur before the tribulation period, and the tribulation period will occur before the millennial kingdom."

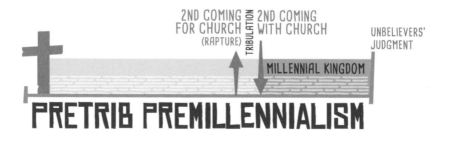

I won't go into great detail about the strengths of the futurist view and the pretrib/premil view. I spent quite a bit of space in my previous books doing that. If you want to study the topic further, please take a look at my Non-Prophet's Guide™ series of books (see the last few pages of this book for more information on those).

THE EXTREMELY RELEVANT
LETTERS TO THE CHURCHES

A number of times in this book, we've discussed the fact that some sections of prophetic scripture have an immediate or literal application as well as secondary applications. For example, we know that certain prophecies related to the first coming of Jesus had dual fulfillments. The prophecy of a virgin giving birth and the prophecy of God calling his Son out of Egypt both had an initial application for the immediate context and a future fulfillment at the time of Christ's first advent.

With that in mind, I'd like to highlight a fascinating point about the churches John addressed in Revelation 2–3. Many prophecy experts agree that the seven churches were not only real churches of that day but represent churches all through the church age. They also say it's possible these churches prophetically foreshadow seven distinct church periods during the church age, and therefore are part of the prophecies of Revelation.

Literal Application

The seven churches John wrote to were literal churches. All of them were located in different areas of modern-day Turkey. The warnings and commendations given to these churches were clearly relevant to those specific churches at that specific time.

Secondary Application

The warnings and commendations to the seven churches also highlight characteristics that can be found in churches at any given time in history. The principles presented can help believers evaluate churches, and even themselves. In this case, chapters 2 and 3 can serve as guardrails and guiding principles that help churches to stay the course and remain faithful to the Lord until he comes again.

Prophetic Application

Finally, the seven churches may also represent seven periods of church history between John's time and the beginning of the tribulation. Some early church leaders believed this would be the case, and history has borne it out as we look through the rearview mirror and the church in our day. The strengths, weaknesses, cultural conditions, and chronology of the seven literal churches John addressed very closely mirror those of the seven chronological stages of church history from John's time until today.

Keep in mind that you will find all seven types of churches in each period of the church age, but a careful study of church history shows that each period is also dominated by one type of church—and the sequence of these dominant types of churches happen to line up in the same order as the seven churches presented in Revelation 2–3. Not all prophecy experts agree on the exact dates or descriptions, but there is quite a broad consensus that this prophetic fulfillment of the seven periods of church history is valid. As with other areas of minor disagreement, no core theologies are affected by opposing views on this topic. Consider the chart below.

CHURCH	KEY FEATURE	CHURCH PERIOD	DATES
Ephesus	Forgot first love	Apostolic (grew legalistic)	AD 30–95
Smyrna	Persecuted	Persecuted (by Rome)	95–300
Pergamum	Adulterous/ worldly	State church (Integrated pagan practices)	312–590
Thyatira	Immorality/ occult	Medieval (Papacy/ occultic/corrupt)	590–1517
Sardis	Alive but dead	Denominational (post-Reformation)	1517–1750
Philadelphia	Alive/thriving	Evangelistic missionary church	1750–1925
Laodicea	Lukewarm	Postmodern	1925–today

WHISKED AWAY

Then at the beginning of chapter 4, we read,

> After this I looked, and there before me was a door standing open
> in heaven. And the voice I had first heard speaking to me like a
> trumpet said, "Come up here, and I will show you what must take
> place after this." At once I was in the Spirit, and there before me
> was a throne in heaven with someone sitting on it (verses 1-2).

Many believe this prophetically points to the rapture occurring at the end
of the church age. After this point in Revelation, there is no mention of the
church on earth during the entire tribulation period. The focus shifts to Israel
and God's judgment of the Babylonian system. This prophetic fulfillment
lines up perfectly with the pretribulation rapture view we have established
throughout this book.

Following the rapture in Revelation 4:1, we spend two chapters in heaven's
throne room. Then in Revelation 6 the tribulation begins with the opening
of the first seal judgment, which brings the rider on the white horse. According
to Daniel 9:27, the evil end-times global leader we commonly refer to as
the antichrist will confirm a covenant between Israel and many. This single
event will officially start the seven-year clock ticking until the physical return
of Christ to earth to set up the millennial kingdom.

CHURCH EVENTS IN HEAVEN

While the tribulation is taking place on earth, the church will experience
two beautiful events in heaven. First, we will attend the bema seat judgment,
or the judgment seat of Christ, to receive rewards for our service to God. Then
we will participate in the marriage supper of the Lamb (Revelation 19:7-10).
There's one more amazing event you and I as church-age believers will experience, but I'll keep this in chronological order and present that later.

During the tribulation period, the world will go through 21 judgments
that range from bad to worse. The effects of the seal judgments will carry into
the trumpet judgments, and the effects of those, in turn, will carry into the
bowl judgments. Prophecy teachers vary on where they place the judgments
during the seven-year time span. I believe the seal and trumpet judgments

will occur during the first half of the tribulation, followed by some key mid-point events, then the bowl judgments will occur during the second half of the period.

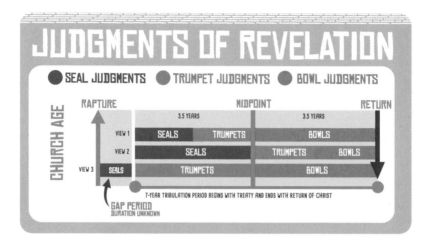

The second half of the tribulation is also known as the great tribulation (Matthew 24:21; see also Daniel 12:1) or the time of Jacob's (Israel's) trouble (Jeremiah 30:7). Revelation 12 and Matthew 24 present various details about how, at the midpoint of the tribulation, Satan and his minions will be cast down to the earth. The enemy will know his time is short, and he will go after the Jewish people with everything he has. If you'll recall from previous chapters, a remnant of the Jewish people will be protected in a place prepared for them for exactly three-and-a-half years.

It is important to remember that one of the key purposes of the tribulation is the salvation of the Jewish nation. The result will be that "all Israel will be saved" (Romans 11:26).

THE ROLLER-COASTER RETURN

I mentioned a moment ago that there is one more incredible event that will take place in heaven while the world is experiencing God's wrath during the tribulation. That event is the return of Christ. We will mount up on white horses, gather behind our Savior, and follow his lead as he pierces the veil between heaven and earth. In a roller coaster-like descent we will cascade down from above and witness Jesus's destruction of the armies of the antichrist with a simple word. In the closing throes of the tribulation period, with the earth completely ravaged and the sun, moon, and stars darkened, the blazing glory of the Lord will pierce the sky as he leads the armies of heaven into the earthly realm.

The armies of the world are gathered in Israel for what they think will be a war against God, but little do they realize they are preparing themselves as a macabre feast for flesh-eating birds. I'll unpack the chronology of events below, but first, use your God-given imagination to envision this scene—and as you do, try to envision it from both the heavenly and earthly perspectives. First, the armies gathered on a darkened battle plain will witness Christ in his full glory suddenly busting through and illuminating the skies. Second, the armies of heaven (which will include you if you have accepted Christ as your Savior) will be behind the Warrior King as part of the most epic procession of all time.

Revelation 19:11-16 describes the scene:

> I saw heaven standing open and there before me was a white horse, whose rider is called Faithful and True. With justice he judges and wages war. His eyes are like blazing fire, and on his head are many crowns. He has a name written on him that no one knows but he himself. He is dressed in a robe dipped in blood, and his name is the Word of God. The armies of heaven were following him, riding on white horses and dressed in fine linen, white and clean. Coming out of his mouth is a sharp sword with which to strike down the nations. "He will rule them with an iron scepter." He treads the winepress of the fury of the wrath of God Almighty. On his robe and on his thigh he has this name written: King of kings and Lord of lords.

Little baby Jesus. Meek and mild Jesus. Grace-filled Jesus. Suffering, submissive Jesus. And at a guaranteed future moment, he will come as the most powerful and righteous conqueror that history, heaven, or earth has ever seen. He is, simply put, King of kings and Lord of lords! Nothing else can compare to him.

AT LONG LAST, THE KINGDOM

As you have seen in this book, the idea of a future golden kingdom age featuring the messianic descendant of David ruling the world from Jerusalem and ushering in a time of global peace is mentioned repeatedly all through the Old Testament. The Psalms, the major and minor prophets, and many passages in the Torah (the first five books of the Old Testament) all contain detailed prophecies about this future kingdom.

We find this theme all through the New Testament as well. One major element of Jesus's teaching on prayer—commonly referred to as the Lord's prayer—is a plea for this future kingdom to be implemented on earth. Right in the middle of this prayer, Jesus said, "Your kingdom come, your will be done, on earth as it is in heaven" (Matthew 6:10). Whether people realize it or not, every time they recite the Lord's prayer, they are praying for Christ's literal, physical kingdom to commence.

The one detail about the millennial kingdom that does not appear in the Old Testament is its duration. God held back this information, which isn't revealed until Revelation 20. There, he informs us six times in the first seven verses that the kingdom age will last 1,000 years.

As mentioned earlier, when God uses symbols, usually they are clearly communicated as symbols and their meanings are given elsewhere in Scripture. Nowhere in Scripture is the number 1,000 symbolic of something else, and there is nothing in the context of Revelation 20 that would suggest that the 1,000-year time frame is to be taken any other way but literally. Furthermore, when the Bible repeats a truth or fact, usually it does so for clarity and impact. Repetition generally tells us that something is important. When God mentions a specific detail six times in seven verses, we should pay attention—especially when it is a detail that has not been revealed for millennia!

So, as we piece all the related texts about the future kingdom age together, here is a snapshot of what that amazing time period will look like. This brief description below doesn't truly do it justice, but I pray it helps paint a basic picture of what the kingdom age will be like.

People

At the end of the tribulation, there will be survivors—including the 144,000 Jewish evangelists, the remnant of Jewish Christians whom Jesus rescues upon his return, and other believers who somehow  make it to the end. These people will enter the millennial kingdom and repopulate the world (Isaiah 65:23). Their life spans will be longer than those of people today—they will live for hundreds of years, just as people did during the preflood era (Isaiah 65:20). Though they will start strong, not all their descendants will accept Christ as Savior, even though he will be literally ruling the world with perfect righteousness (Isaiah 11:4, 9; 51:4).

Those of us who will be caught up in the rapture will spend seven years with the Lord in heaven, return with him, and serve him as he sets up the millennial kingdom. We will enter the kingdom with the glorified bodies that we receive at the rapture/resurrection. We (like the angels) will not be married or even have a desire to be married (Matthew 22:30; Mark 12:25). We will help the Lord govern the world in its new state (Luke 22:30; Revelation 5:10). This next detail is really amazing to me: Old Testament-era believers will be raised from the dead at the beginning of the millennium, and we church-age believers will partner with them as we rule with Jesus (Daniel 12:1-2; see also Isaiah 26:19; Ezekiel 37:13-14)! More on this below.

Animals

If you've ever studied the animal world, or if you have watched any nature documentaries about life in the wild, you've surely seen how brutal and unforgiving the animal kingdom is. This was not the original state of the world or God's intention. The fall corrupted all of creation. This aspect of the curse will be removed during the millennial kingdom, and you'll be happy to know there will be no carnivores or poisonous animals on earth during that time. No animals will ever want to eat or attack you. The earth will return to conditions similar to those that existed before the fall (Isaiah 11:6-9).

Earth

When Christ sets up the millennial kingdom, the earth as a whole will be renovated, updated, and fixed. Humankind and nature will live in harmony as originally intended (Isaiah 2:2; 11:6-9; Zechariah 14:8), and  the geography of the world will change for the better. Jerusalem—the historical epicenter of God's prophecies and activities—will become the highest point on earth. I'm looking forward to a world with no poison ivy, thorns, ticks, or mosquitoes! If the last two still exist in the kingdom, I'm sure they will only bite plants.

Government

Jesus will rule the entire world, which is what sin-filled rulers have tried to do all through history. Evil figures from Nimrod to Hitler to the future antichrist will have acted upon their aspirations to rule the earth, and will have failed, leaving carnage and destruction in their wake. All that will come to an end when the rightful and righteous King sits on his throne in Jerusalem and governs with complete righteousness (Jeremiah 23:5; Isaiah 9:7; 33:22; Matthew 19:28; 25:31; 1 Timothy 6:15; Revelation 17:14; 20:4).

Church-age believers and Old Testament believers will help Jesus rule the nations (Revelation 2:26-27; 20:4), judge the world (1 Corinthians 6:2), and will be "a chosen people, a royal priesthood, a holy nation" (1 Peter 2:9). Some Bible expositors suggest that we will be given more or less authority and responsibility in the millennial kingdom depending on how we managed opportunities and responsibilities during our lifetime on earth (Luke 19:11-27).

FINALLY, ETERNITY

Like any good book, story, or movie, the resolution of the world's greatest narrative just gets better and better. It would be enough for God to take his bride in the rapture. It would be enough to give church-age believers rewards at the bema seat. It would be enough for believers to attend the wedding supper of the Lamb. It would be enough to return with Jesus on air-gliding heavenly horses. It would be more than enough for us to join with resurrected Old Testament saints and rule with Christ in the millennial kingdom. But after all of that, there's something even more magnificent that we will experience because of what Jesus did for us on the cross.

In Revelation chapter 21, John describes "a new heaven and a new earth" (verse 1). Along with this new heaven and new earth will come a new Jerusalem, which was referred to in the book of Hebrews as a heavenly city that Abraham was looking forward to. It is also (I believe) the very same place Jesus spoke of when he said he was going to prepare a place for us (John 14:2-3).

So, as has been the pattern in the last few chapters of Revelation, we are given new details that generations of believers have longed to know. These details are provided at the end of God's revealed Word. All of Revelation 21 and the first five verses of Revelation 22 are worth taking the time to read slowly and carefully. Our future is glorious beyond imagination!

I have always found it interesting that John used 14 chapters to describe details of what will take place during the seven-year tribulation, but only one-third of a chapter to describe the 1,000-year kingdom and just a bit more than one chapter to describe eternity. God has more amazing surprises for us that have yet to be revealed—surprises that we will enjoy forever!

No wonder 1 Corinthians 2:9 informs us that "eye has not seen, nor ear heard, nor have entered into the heart of man the things which God has prepared for those who love Him" (NKJV). We can't even imagine what eternity with God will be like—our minds don't possess the capacity. Nothing we have ever seen, heard, or imagined comes close to how amazing our new habitation will be.

That should give us great encouragement and help us to push through our present struggles, which "are not worth comparing with the glory that will be revealed in us" (Romans 8:18). Knowing that we have all this to look forward to should help us persevere through our "light and momentary troubles" (2 Corinthians 4:17).

FOR OUR LIGHT AND MOMENTARY TROUBLES ARE ACHIEVING FOR US AN ETERNAL GLORY THAT FAR OUTWEIGHS THEM ALL.
2 CORINTHIANS 4:17

CHAPTER 15

The 800-Pound End-Times Gorilla in the Room

You've made it this far—congratulations for studying the entire Bible through the lens of prophecy! I pray this has been an eye-opening journey for you. As with most in-depth systematic studies, I suspect you've had some questions answered and even more questions raised. Good! Studying Scripture is an incredible lifelong journey for every believer who engages in it.

So, how does this newfound head knowledge translate into real-world application? Here's how: I believe that now, more than any other time in history, people need answers. We're in a new era. People all across the planet are witness to the global instability of this fallen world. Things were precarious and unstable before, but in today's post COVID-19 world, it seems humanity has been plunged into a controlled free fall toward collapse. How's that for encouragement?

That may be a hard pill to swallow. It may seem extreme. I'm not saying the world is going to end tomorrow, but I am saying that apart from God sovereignly holding things together until his appointed time, this world is toast.

Right now, the 800-pound gorilla in the room is the condition of the world. The convulsions of nature, the moral and spiritual corruption all around us, the widespread deception and delusional thinking that pervades society, the cultural and political results of COVID-19, the geopolitical instability all around the globe, the impending financial collapse, the coarsening of culture, the apostasy in the church, and the rapid growth of the occult are all conditions that weigh heavily on the hearts of discerning believers today.

We have a front-row seat to all that is taking place. A lost and dying world is asking the big questions of eternal significance. So how do we who are believers respond? How can we live with hope and joy in a rapidly decaying world? How can we light up the dark with the hope of the gospel? How can we reach the lost people whom God loves when they are hearing so many competing and deceptive voices?

I want to end this book by giving you three practical steps that I pray will help equip you for your calling at this special moment in history.

PRACTICAL STEP #1— PUT ON YOUR OXYGEN MASK FIRST

If you have ever flown on a plane, you've heard the instructions about what to do when the cabin loses air pressure. When the oxygen masks drop from the ceiling, you are to put your mask on first before helping others put on their masks. I've always been struck by how nonchalant these instructions sound. It's as if what the airline personnel are really saying is, "If something breaks a hole in this plane and all the air gets sucked out, we hope that the thin, plastic oxygen masks will still work. If so, put yours on first so you don't pass out before you can strap this lifesaving gadget onto your face."

The reason I use that analogy is because in a life-or-death situation, you are of no help to anyone else if you are not okay. So I ask you: Are you okay?

These are trying times. First, we need to make sure we are spiritually and emotionally healthy. Otherwise, we're no good to anyone else. That's not being selfish; it's being realistic.

The prophet Elijah hit the wall of depression after a huge victory, and the Lord put him on the path to recovery by telling him to rest and eat (1 Kings 19:7-8). In the Psalms, David cried out repeatedly to the Lord in the midst of depression and despair. Job poured his heart out to God and was as raw and real as you can get.

So how do we stay positive, sane, and laser-focused on our calling during such disruptive times? By turning to God's prophetic Word. Here is a checklist of God's faithful promises that you can review daily—or anytime you need to reboot your perspective after hearing the news.

> God will never leave you (Hebrews 13:5).
>
> Mortals cannot overrule God's work in your life (Hebrews 13:6).
>
> If God is for you, no one can be against you (Romans 8:31).
>
> Jesus will be with you to the very end of the age (Matthew 28:20).
>
> You were put here at this time by God (Psalm 139:13).
>
> Every day of your life is sovereignly directed by the Lord (Psalm 139:16).
>
> God will give you what you need when you need it (Philippians 4:19).
>
> Every struggle you face is worthwhile (2 Corinthians 4:17).
>
> The joy of the Lord is your strength as you work (Nehemiah 8:10).
>
> Keep the main thing the main thing (Matthew 28:19).
>
> God will lead you through unfamiliar territory (Isaiah 42:16).
>
> Jesus will be with you in life's storms (Matthew 14:25; Mark 4:38).
>
> Jesus is coming soon, and his reward is with him (Revelation 22:12).
>
> God is still on the throne (Psalm 11:4).

MAKE DISCIPLES
MATTHEW 28:19

I know it is overwhelming at times to watch all that is happening in this world, but it is also an extreme privilege! Check out 1 Peter 1:10-12, which points out the fact that we are a privileged generation. Back in chapter 13, I mentioned that there was one more prophetic passage from 1 Peter that I wanted to share, and this is it:

> Concerning this salvation, the prophets, who spoke of the grace that was to come to you, searched intently and with the greatest care, trying to find out the time and circumstances to which the Spirit of Christ in them was pointing when he predicted the sufferings of the Messiah and the glories that would follow. It was revealed to them that they were not serving themselves but you, when they spoke of the things that have now been told you by those who have preached the gospel to you by the Holy Spirit sent from heaven. Even angels long to look into these things.

First, notice that the prophets who wrote much of the Old Testament desperately wanted to understand the timing and the signs of the Messiah's coming. Second, they wanted to understand the prophecies related to both the sufferings (the cross) and the glories that would follow (the kingdom age). And third, even angels long to look into these things!

So when you find yourself feeling overwhelmed by the news of the day, remind yourself that God is still on the throne, that we are a privileged generation, and that even the prophets and angels longed to see what is right in front of us!

PRACTICAL STEP #2—
GIVE OXYGEN TO OTHERS

In golf terms, God has teed it up for us to preach the gospel with a sense of urgency and intentionality. You may not have a pulpit, but you can still preach—in multiple ways. You can preach by how you live your life. You can preach by how you build relationships and tell people what Jesus has done in your life. You can preach by how you respond to others on social media. You can preach by how you trust God in the middle of the storm. You can preach by how you serve others calmly while the world is falling apart. You can preach.

You may not fill stadiums, but you can ask God to send you people whom he wants to reach. I dare you to pray that and see what God does next. Often, we assume no one will listen to us. I'm not talking about going out on a street corner with a bullhorn and a sign, but we can ask God to show us who to reach in our everyday social circles. We can ask God to send to us those who need to hear the gospel. And we can ask God to guide us as we endeavor to point people to the Savior.

Perhaps God will lead you to give this book to someone. Perhaps you are that someone who received this book as a gift. If that is the case, I want to make sure you do not put this book down until you have heard about how to be saved through the sacrificial death of Christ. You can't earn salvation. None of us are good enough to obtain it. Salvation is a gift. Jesus paid it all. We need only to receive the gift and put our trust in Jesus alone for salvation. Here is a simple way to understand it—I use this outline in all of my books. It is so simple a child can understand it, and it is so profound that it can change the direction of your life and your eternal destination.

One does not become a Christian by following a formula, but I've found that what I'm about to share is an effective way to explain what it means to receive Christ and become a true Christian. It's as simple as A, B, C.

Admit that you are a sinner. No one is perfect. We all fall short. Romans 3:23 says, "All have sinned and fall short of the glory of God." Romans 6:23 says, "The wages [payment] of sin is death, but the gift of God is eternal life in Christ Jesus our Lord."

Believe that Jesus is God's Son and that he died on the cross with your sins on him. Romans 5:8 says, "While we were still sinners, Christ died for us."

CONFESS

Confess Jesus as your Lord. This doesn't mean you will never mess up again. Rather, it means you desire to serve him and learn his ways as you grow spiritually. Romans 10:9 says, "If you confess with your mouth the Lord Jesus and believe in your heart that God has raised Him from the dead, you will be saved" (NKJV).

Below is a simple prayer you can pray. These words aren't magical. Again, this is not a formula. But if these words accurately reflect the state of your heart, then when you pray this prayer, you will become a Christian. You will have placed your faith in Christ, and he will forgive your sins. As a believer, you will be able to look forward to eternity with Jesus in heaven, and you will avoid the terrible time of tribulation that will soon come upon the world. Pray this prayer now:

> Lord Jesus, I admit that I am a sinner. I have sinned against you, and sin separates me from you. I thank you that you died on the cross for me. You took my sins upon you and paid my penalty at the cross. I believe you are who you say you are—God in human flesh. I believe you died for my sins. I want to accept your gift of salvation and, at this moment, I ask you to be my Savior. I thank you for your forgiveness. I now have new life. I now claim you as my Savior and my Lord. In your name, amen.

If you just prayed that prayer, you are a new creation. The Bible tells us that heaven is celebrating right now because of your decision. The Holy Spirit now indwells you and will guide you and keep you. You won't be perfect, but you are forgiven, and Jesus will never leave you. His work in you has just begun. You are an adopted co-heir with Christ. You will one day live and reign with him in the millennial kingdom and forever in eternity. Welcome to the family of God!

PRACTICAL STEP #3—
FINISH STRONG

I'd like to share my personal mission statement with you. It is simple so I can remember it, but the concepts are powerful, and most importantly, biblical. These four simple statements guide my choices, outlook, plans, and focus. Perhaps they will encourage you as you read them.

Follow God.

Love people.

Live fully.

Finish strong.

Those simple statements—in the context of biblical priorities and devotion to Christ—guide everything I do. I don't do them perfectly or even consistently, but they guide me nonetheless. They are reminders of my calling and my need for growth. They guide my next steps as a disciple of Christ and they help keep me on track. Here's why I share them: Do the first three commitments matter much if we neglect the fourth?

Whatever your personal mission statement or guiding-life verse might be, what does it matter if you don't finish strong? How many ministries, marriages, careers, and relationships have you seen fail after appearing successful on the first three points?

What difference do the first three commitments make if our legacy is ruined by moral compromise or worldly pursuits? Or, as Jesus so aptly put it in Matthew 16:26, "What good will it be for someone to gain the whole world, yet forfeit their soul?"

In the context of finishing strong, I will ask a similar question. What good will our life's work be if we throw it all away for earthly, temporary things? My fellow Christian, I know you are tired and weary at times. But if there's one thing we can learn from this chronological study of prophecy, it is that God is a promise-keeper. Every single statement he has made about our future will come to pass exactly as he has promised. Keep fighting. Keep putting your oxygen mask on. Keep giving others oxygen. And most importantly, finish strong! Jesus is coming soon, and his reward is with him.

> Therefore, since we are surrounded by such a great cloud of witnesses, let us throw off everything that hinders and the sin that so easily entangles. And let us run with perseverance the race marked out for us, fixing our eyes on Jesus, the pioneer and perfecter of faith. For the joy set before him he endured the cross, scorning its shame, and sat down at the right hand of the throne of God. Consider him who endured such opposition from sinners, so that you will not grow weary and lose heart.
>
> —HEBREWS 12:1-3

NOTES

1. "Apollo 13 timeline: The hectic days of NASA's 'successful failure' to the moon," *All About Space*, April 11, 2020, https://www.space.com/apollo-13-timeline.html.

2. Roy B. Zuck, *Basic Bible Interpretation* (Colorado Springs, CO: David C. Cook, 1991), 175.

3. "Will human knowledge soon have the power to double every 12 hours?," *Glenn Beck*, April 7, 2014, https://www.glennbeck.com/2014/04/07/will-human-knowledge-soon-have-the-power-to-double-every-12-hours/.

Other Great Reading
by Todd Hampson

The Non-Prophet's Guide™ to the End Times

Do you tend to avoid studying books of the Bible like Revelation and Ezekiel? Does it feel like words such as *rapture* and *apocalypse* fly right over your head? It's common to dismiss these and other topics related to Bible prophecy as irrelevant and…well…too complicated.

But God's Word says, "Blessed is the one who reads aloud the words of this prophecy, and blessed are those who hear it and take to heart what is written in it, because the time is near" (Revelation 1:3).

Prepare to be blessed in a meaningful way! *The Non-Prophet's Guide™ to the End Times* combines engaging illustrations with down-to-earth explanations to help you navigate the ins and outs of Bible prophecy. There's no better time to grasp God's plans for the future—and for you—than this very moment.

The Non-Prophet's Guide™ to the End Times Workbook

Dig deeper into what the Bible says about the end times and gain insight into God's plan for your future. Todd Hampson's companion workbook to his bestselling *The Non-Prophet's Guide™ to the End Times* makes the challenging study of Bible prophecy clear, understandable, and fun.

With more than 100 helpful and humorous graphics and illustrations, you can explore scriptural prophecies and discover answers for your questions about the last days, such as…

- How does fulfilled Bible prophecy affect our view of prophecies not yet fulfilled?
- What can we learn from those who were watching at Jesus's first coming?
- How can we discern between conspiracy theories and trustworthy facts that line up with end-time geopolitical signs?

The Non-Prophet's Guide™ to the Book of Revelation

If the final book of the Bible has ever left you scratching your head or wondering what to make of plagues and horsemen, your friendly Non-Prophet is here to help you read Revelation as never before.

Full of engaging graphics, author and illustrator Todd Hampson has created a user-friendly guide to John's prophecies about the last days. This concise and appealing study

- removes the fear factor and demystifies the capstone book of the Bible
- provides biblical clarity about the key events in the end times
- helps reclaim your hope, confidence, and joy in the promised future

The Non-Prophet's Guide™ to the Book of Revelation offers informative study tools for understanding its prophecies, and practical challenges to apply God's truths to your life today.

The Non-Prophet's Guide™ to Spiritual Warfare

Even as a Christian, it can be difficult to discern the facts about the supernatural nature of good and evil. How much has pop culture influenced our ideas about angels and demons? Why do we as Christians face spiritual warfare when the Holy Spirit dwells within us? What limits exist on Satan's powers?

In *The Non-Prophet's Guide™ to Spiritual Warfare*, bestselling author and illustrator Todd Hampson gets to the heart of your questions about spiritual battles, angels, demons, the nature of evil, and more. With Todd's signature combination of light-hearted illustrations and thoughtful applications of Scripture, this guide is both easy to understand and deeply informative.

You will learn to...

- discern between cultural myths and biblical facts about the supernatural
- recognize the real threats you face while remaining grounded in God's truth
- understand why being ready to stand against demonic influence is more important now than ever before

The Non-Prophet's Guide™ to Spiritual Warfare will give you the resources you need to champion spiritual battles, while inspiring you to dive deeper into God's Word to equip yourself with truth.

The Non-Prophet's Guide™ to the Bible

The world's all-time bestseller, the Bible, is truly unique: an ancient collection of 66 separate books written across 1,500 years that fits together like a perfectly crafted puzzle. It proclaims itself to be the Word of God—and supports this claim with hundreds of specific, now-fulfilled prophecies.

Because of its massive cultural impact, readers of all backgrounds and beliefs ask questions about the Bible's context, history, purpose, and reliability. Enter *The Non-Prophet's Guide™ to the Bible*: a bright, infographic-packed panorama designed to give you

- a section-by-section overview of the Bible, illuminating each book's distinct role in telling God's story

- a crash course on who wrote the Scriptures, when they were written, and how they were preserved through the ages

- the compelling case for why you can believe the Bible truly is the Word of God

Whether you're a longtime believer looking to better understand Scripture or an interested newcomer seeking answers about Christianity, this accessible guide provides the insight and information you need to see how the Bible portrays a global history that has unfolded in the direction of God's promises.